ソォーリー　パーパニ

D1191474

Reading and Writing

JAPANESE

EDITORIAL STAFF

FLORENCE SAKADE : *General Editor*
KENJI EMORI : *Associate Editor (Japanese Language)*
RALPH FRIEDRICH : *Associate Editor (English Language)*
SUSUMU OHASHI : *Assistant Editor*

A Guide to

READING & WRITING

JAPANESE

当用漢字

The 1,850 Basic Characters
and the Kana Syllabaries

Revised Edition

CHARLES E. TUTTLE COMPANY
Rutland, Vermont & Tokyo, Japan

European Representatives

For the Continent:
BOXERBOOKS, INC., *Zurich*

For the British Isles:
PRENTICE-HALL INTERNATIONAL, INC., *London*

Published by the Charles E. Tuttle Company
of Rutland, Vermont & Tokyo, Japan
with editorial offices at
15 Edogawa-cho, Bunkyo-ku, Tokyo

Copyright in Japan, 1959
by Charles E. Tuttle Co.

Library of Congress
Catalog Card No. 59–10412

First edition, 1959
Four reprintings
Second edition (revised), 1962
Second printing, 1962

Printed in Japan

TABLE OF CONTENTS

INTRODUCTION

THIS BOOK is designed for those who are eager to acquaint themselves with the written Japanese language and to acquire an elementary ability to read and write it. It has been the purpose of the editor to produce, in as practical a form as possible, a handbook that will furnish the beginner in written Japanese with the knowledge of sufficient characters to enable him to read and write the language in its everyday style. Specifically, the book presents the 1,850 characters prescribed by the Japanese Ministry of Education and adopted by law as those most essential for common use and everyday communication. Since Japanese publications in general now limit themselves to the use of these 1,850 characters (except in the case of proper names), it is no longer a formidable task for the student of the written language to learn to read ordinary books and periodicals and to write in reasonably fluent style. It should be noted that the editor has made a positive effort to include in this volume only the most useful definitions of the *kanji* themselves and the most practical examples of their use in everyday words.

The book is divided into two major sections. The first of these presents the 881 characters designated by the Ministry of Education as the basic requirement for the six years of elementary school. The choice of these characters and their order of appearance in the list were determined by the Ministry through careful research into the frequency of their use, and the resulting selection thus represents the minimum of characters considered essential for common use. Similarly, the majority of the compounds given are those which the Ministry's most recent research shows to be of high frequency in everyday use.

The second major section of the book presents the 1,850 charac-

7

ters designated as "standard" for general everyday use in the publishing world. They include, of course, the 881 basic characters, and the total represents the most significant measure taken to date to simplify the written Japanese language. Not only do these 1,850 characters represent a major reduction in the number formerly in general use; they also represent a simplification of readings and, in a number of cases, of written forms. It should be of considerable interest to foreign students of Japanese to know that many words formerly written with *kanji* (characters) are now written with *kana* (phonetic symbols), that numerous abstruse readings of individual characters have been discarded, and that many of the characters themselves have been simplified from their earlier complex forms. The editor of this book has further assisted the process of simplification for the foreign student by omitting occasional readings that are considered too specialized or too uncommon for the beginner in *kanji*.

It is pertinent to note that the process of simplification is being continued in Japan. In the "Proposed Changes" section of this book will be found one group of 28 characters destined for probable elimination from the standard list and another group of 28 considered for inclusion. These proposed changes, although not yet legally sanctioned, have already been adopted by publishers. In the same section of the book will be found a list of new readings and writings proposed for adoption. It should be added that *kana* usage, particularly as it affects *okurigana* (word endings written in phonetic symbols), is still undergoing revision. These matters notwithstanding, the contents of the present volume are as up-to-date as it has been possible to make them.

The 881 essential characters are given with their *on-yomi* (readings taken from Chinese), *kun-yomi* (native Japanese readings), definitions, and number of strokes. Each character is accompanied by a chart showing the proper order of strokes in its writing. The listing of characters follows that of the graded list established by the Ministry of Education. The readings are those designated for use in the elementary grades. Each character is followed by compounds that illustrate its use in the formation of everyday words.

The 1,850 general-use characters are presented with their *on-yomi*, *kun-yomi*, and definitions, but without illustrative compounds. In

8

many cases, however, they may be found in compound form in examples given for the 881 essential characters. The order of listing for the general-use characters is that of the number of strokes, in accordance with the latest Ministry of Education list. Since it would be superfluous to repeat the readings and definitions of the 881 essential characters when they appear in the general-use list, each is indicated only by its proper number in the list and the number of the page where it may be found in the list of essential characters.

It should be mentioned here that in 1951 the Ministry of Education found it necessary to supplement the list of 1,850 characters with a list of 92 characters approved for use in personal names. Although this supplementary list is not included in the present volume, the story of its adoption is of interest. After the original standard list had been approved by law, it was discovered that a number of characters traditionally used in personal names had been excluded. The situation that resulted had its amusing side. Parents who had chosen among the excluded characters in selecting names for their newborn children were met with refusal when they sought to register the births at government offices, since the characters were missing from the approved list. Because the majority of these parents countered with a refusal on their own part to substitute characters from the approved list, a sizable number of young Japanese citizens remained legally nameless. To provide an escape from this intolerable predicament, the Ministry of Education came to the rescue by issuing its supplementary list of 92 name characters.

In an effort to include as many useful words as possible, the editor has largely excluded proper nouns and has attempted to avoid duplication among the examples of words given. Some repetitions were inevitable, however, because of the limited use of certain *kanji*. As far as possible, three examples of combinations have been provided for each of the 881 essential *kanji*, but in some cases—either because the *kanji* are limited in use or because fewer examples suffice (as with numerals)—fewer examples are given. It should be noted that a few of the *kanji*, including those of Japanese rather than Chinese origin, have no *on-yomi* (e.g., Nos. 302 and 749), while certain others have no *kun-yomi* (e.g., Nos. 155 and 444).

A few words regarding romanization and pronunciation are in

order. The Hepburn system of romanization has been followed through-out, for the simple reason that it is the least confusing to foreign students of Japanese and is the most frequently used. The change of *n* to *m* before *b*, *m*, and *p* in spoken Japanese is indicated by the use of *m* in the romanized spellings, e.g., *sambyaku* (three hundred), *sammyaku* (mountain range), *dempō* (telegram). Where correct pronunciation and word-meaning require a careful distinction between syllables, a hyphen indicates the proper separation, e.g., *sen-en* (one thousand yen), *kao-iro* (complexion), *i-in* (committee member), *ashi-ato* (foot-print), *shin-ya* (midnight). The hyphen is also used to mark off the honorific *o* and the prefix *ō* meaning "large" or "great," e.g., *o-kane* (money), *ō-ame* (heavy rain). The change from an unvoiced to a voiced consonant (*dakuon*) in word combinations is shown, wherever possible, in brackets in the readings for the 881 essential *kanji*.

The following examples explain the typographical arrangements used in giving the readings and definitions of the characters:

> KEN; *mi(ru)*, to see, to look
>> *On-yomi* in capitals, *kun-yomi* in italics, definitions in roman.
>> *Okurigana* of *kun-yomi* in parentheses.
>
> SAN [ZAN]; *yama*, mountain
>> Vocalized (*dakuon*) form of *on-yomi* in brackets, *kun-yomi* in italics.
>
> SHIN; *kokoro* [*gokoro*], heart, spirit, mind
>> Vocalized (*dakuon*) form of *kun-yomi* in brackets.
>
> GEN, GAN; *moto*, beginning, foundation
>> Two *on-yomi* of same meaning.
>
> KATSU (energy)
>> No *kun-yomi*. Original meaning of character given in parentheses.
>
> I (easy); EKI, divination
>> Two *on-yomi* of different meaning. Original meaning of character given in parentheses. No *kun-yomi*.
>
> HI, ratio, comparison; *kura(beru)*, to compare
>> Definitions immediately following *on-yomi* indicate that it is used either independently or in compounds. *Okurigana* of *kun-yomi* in parentheses.

10

Although there are exceptions to the rule, *on-yomi* are usually used in compounds. In cases where *on-yomi* can be used either independently or in compounds, effort has been made to distinguish this fact insofar as possible by placing the definition of the *on-yomi* immediately after it, preceded by a comma.

A few basic rules will suffice to explain the proper method of writing Japanese characters. In general, the basic rule in the order of strokes is from

1. top to bottom:

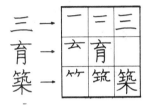

2. left to right:

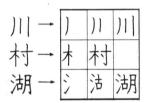

Other rules are

3. When two or more strokes cross, horizontal strokes usually precede perpendicular ones:

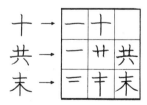

4. Sometimes perpendicular strokes precede horizontal ones:

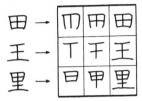

5. Center first, then left and right:

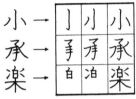

6. Perpendicular line running through center written last:

7. Right-to-left diagonal stroke precedes left-to-right:

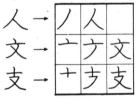

8. Constant effort should be made to keep the characters of uniform size.

In this book, characters of nine strokes or less are drawn stroke by stroke. For purposes of simplification, characters requiring more than nine strokes are shown with one or more of their component elements already drawn, e.g., No. 370, in which the terminal "mouth" simply reproduces in smaller size the character *kuchi* (No. 27). In these cases, an element already drawn is shown in small type under the compounds along with the number of the original character. If the element already drawn is not a character itself, it is shown in small type along with a character in which its stroke order has been previously shown.

It should be noted, however, that when one character (usually in reduced size) is used to form part of a more complex character, the shape of the former sometimes changes. Thus No. 15, for example, changes from 木 to 扌 when it becomes a part of No. 107 村. Other examples are the change of 人 to 亻 in 休 and of 手 to 扌 in 打. Changes of this kind are also shown in small type under the compounds. Although there are partial differences in the accepted writings of *kanji*, the forms shown in this book are those approved for use in textbooks; in 1961 these forms will become universal for all textbooks. Printed forms, of course, may differ somewhat from written forms.

The book concludes with instructions for writing the two *kana* syllabaries, *hiragana* (phonetic symbols in cursive style, used principally for native words and word endings) and *katakana* (phonetic symbols in angular style, used chiefly for transcribing foreign words). The syllabaries are accompanied by a chart listing sound changes and *kana* combinations with their romanized forms.

The models for the writing of the characters are the work of Mr. Kenji Emori, expert calligrapher and official of the Elementary and Secondary Education Division, Ministry of Education. In addition to his responsibility for assessing the calligraphic and art content of all school textbooks submitted for the Ministry's approval, he has been engaged in an intensive study of the form, style, and stroke order of *kanji*. Valuable assistance in the preparation of the book was also given by Mr. Susumu Ōhashi and Mr. Ralph Friedrich, who participated in selecting the English definitions and checking the accuracy of the manuscript. The editor further acknowledges her indebtedness to the following texts compiled by the Ministry of Education: *Hitsujun no Tebiki*, *Shōgakkō Gakushū Shidō Yōryō*, *Kokugo Series Nos. 21 and 33*, and *Kyōiku Kanji no Gakunen Haitō*.

NOTE TO THE REVISED EDITION

IN RESPONSE to requests from many users of this book who have wanted to use it for a dictionary as well as for a study guide, an index of the Japanese readings of the characters has been added at the end. So the book now has two dictionary uses: (1) If the character is known, look for it by stroke-count in the list of 1,850 general-use characters (including the 881 essential characters) beginning on page 192. (2) If the reading but not the character is known, consult the index beginning on page 288. As it has proved impractical to include an index of English equivalents, if neither the character nor the reading is known, recourse must be had to one of the many English-Japanese dictionaries.

Keep in mind that the following 881 characters are not arranged in order suitable for dictionary use (they can, however, be found easily by either of the steps described above) but in an order determined by the Japanese Ministry of Education after careful research into the frequency of their use and recommended for teaching in elementary schools. This order is most valuable in indicating the relative importance of the characters and a suggested priority to be followed in their study. They are divided by school grades as follows:

School Grade	Character Numbers
1	1–46
2	47–151
3	152–338
4	339–543
5	544–737
6	738–881

Dover? Numbers refer to Wieger: Chinese Characters

The 881
ESSENTIAL CHARACTERS

一	一			**ICHI**, *hito(tsu)*, one 一月 *ichigatsu*, January 一番 *ichiban*, first, best 一冊 *issatsu*, one (book, magazine)
1 1 stroke				
二	一	二		**NI**, *futa(tsu)*, two 二月 *nigatsu*, February 二か月 *nikagetsu*, two months 二回 *nikai*, twice
2 2 strokes				
三	一	二	三	**SAN**, *mi*, *mit(tsu)*, three 三月 *sangatsu*, March 三人 *sannin*, three people 三日 *mikka*, three days, the third day
3 3 strokes				
四	丶	冂	冂	**SHI**, *yon*, *yo*, *yot(tsu)*, four 四月 *shigatsu*, April 四日 *yokka*, four days, the fourth day 四十 *shijū*, *yonjū*, forty
	四	四		
4 5 strokes				

15

五	一	丁	五	GO, *itsu(tsu)*, five
	五			五月 *gogatsu*, May 五人 *gonin*, five people 五十 *gojū*, fifty
5 4 strokes				

六	`	亠	六	ROKU, *mut(tsu)*, six
	六			六月 *rokugatsu*, June 六か月 *rokkagetsu*, six months 六十 *rokujū*, sixty
6 4 strokes				

七	一	七		SHICHI, *nana(tsu)*, seven
				七月 *shichigatsu*, July 七か月 *nanakagetsu*, seven months 七十 *shichijū, nanajū*, seventy
7 2 strokes				

八	ノ	八		HACHI, *yat(tsu)*, eight
				八月 *hachigatsu*, August 八か月 *hachikagetsu*, eight months 八十 *hachijū*, eighty
8 2 strokes				

九	ノ	九		KU, KYŪ, *kokono(tsu)*, nine
				九月 *kugatsu*, September 九十 *kujū, kyūjū*, ninety 九時 *kuji*, nine o'clock
9 2 strokes				

16

十	一	十		JŪ, *tō*, ten 十月 *jūgatsu*, October 十日 *tōka*, ten days, the tenth day 十回 *jikkai*, ten times
10 2 strokes				

日	丨	冂	月		NICHI, JITSU; *hi* [*bi*], day, sun; ~*ka*, suffix for counting days 日曜日 *nichiyōbi*, Sunday 昨日 *sakujitsu*, yesterday 朝日 *asahi*, morning sun
	日				
11 4 strokes					

月	丿	刀	月		GETSU, GATSU; *tsuki* [*zuki*], month, moon 月曜日 *getsuyōbi*, Monday 来月 *raigetsu*, next month 三日月 *mikazuki*, new moon
	月				
12 4 strokes					

火	丶	丷	少		KA; *hi* [*bi*], fire 火曜日 *kayōbi*, Tuesday 火ばち *hibachi*, charcoal brazier 火事 *kaji*, fire, conflagration
	火				
13 4 strokes		火			

水	丿	丮	水		SUI; *mizu*, water 大水 *ō-mizu*, flood, inundation 水力 *suiryoku*, water power 水兵 *suihei*, sailor
	水				
14 4 strokes					

木	一	十	才	MOKU, BOKU; *ki* [*gi*], tree, wood
	木			木曜日　*mokuyōbi*, Thursday 材木　*zaimoku*, lumber 木製　*mokusei*, made of wood
15 4 strokes				朩

金	ノ	入	全	KIN, gold; KON (gold); *kane*, money
	仐	仝	余	金曜日　*kin-yōbi*, Friday お金　*o-kane*, money 金魚　*kingyo*, goldfish
16 8 strokes	金	金		釒

土	一	十	土	DO, TO; *tsuchi*, earth, soil
				土曜日　*doyōbi*, Saturday 土地　*tochi*, ground, plot of land 土人　*dojin*, native
17 3 strokes				圡

左	一	ナ	左	SA; *hidari*, left
	左	左		左派　*saha*, leftist (political), left wing 左側　*sasoku*, *hidarigawa*, left side
18 5 strokes				左手　*hidarite*, left hand

右	ノ	ナ	大	YŪ, U; *migi*, right
	右	右		左右　*sayū*, left and right 右派　*uha*, right wing (political) 右側　*usoku*, *migigawa*, right side
19 5 strokes				

上	丨	卜	上	JŌ; *ue*, top, above, on; *kami*, upper; *nobo(ru)*, to go up, to go toward Tōkyō; *a(geru)*, to raise; *a-(garu)*, to rise
20 3 strokes				上流 *jōryū*, upstream, upper class 海上 *kaijō*, on the sea, maritime 川上 *kawakami*, upstream

下	一	丁	下	KA, GE; *shita*, bottom, under, beneath; *moto*, base; *shimo*, lower; *kuda(ru)*, to go down, to go away from Tōkyō; *sa(geru)*, to hang (v.t.), to lower; *sa(garu)*, to hang down
21 3 strokes				川下 *kawashimo*, downstream 下品 *gehin*, vulgar, coarse 地下鉄 *chikatetsu*, subway

大	一	ナ	大	DAI, TAI; *ō(kii)*, big, large, great
22 3 strokes				大学 *daigaku*, university, college 大変 *taihen*, tremendous, serious 大広間 *ō-hiroma*, grand hall

中	丶	⼞	⼝	CHŪ; *naka*, middle, within, inside
	中			中学校 *chūgakkō*, middle school 中心 *chūshin*, center, heart (of a city, etc.)
23 4 strokes				集中 *shūchū*, concentration

小	亅	丿	小	SHŌ; *ko, o, chii(sai)*, small, minor
24 3 strokes				小学校 *shōgakkō*, primary school 小屋 *koya*, hut 小説 *shōsetsu*, novel (fiction)

19

目	丨	冂	冃		MOKU; *me*, eye; also used as an ordinal suffix
	冃	目			横目　　*yokome*, side glance 目的　　*mokuteki*, purpose 目標　　*mokuhyō*, mark, target
25 5 strokes					
耳	一	丆	丅		JI; *mimi*, ear
	𦥑	王	耳		早耳　　*hayamimi*, keen of hearing　　「ears 耳鳴り　*miminari*, ringing in the 耳が遠い　*mimi ga tōi*, deaf
26 6 strokes					耳
口	丶	冂	口		KŌ, KU; *kuchi* [*guchi*], mouth
					口ひげ　*kuchihige*, mustache 入口　　*iriguchi*, entrance 口論　　*kōron*, dispute
27 3 strokes					口
手	ノ	亠	三		SHU; *te*, hand
	手				握手　*akushu*, handshake 手袋　*tebukuro*, gloves 手紙　*tegami*, letter
28 4 strokes					扌
足	丶	冂	口		SOKU [ZOKU]; *ashi*, foot, leg; *ta(riru)*, to be sufficient
	𤴡	足	足		足跡　*ashi-ato*, footprint 満足　*manzoku*, satisfaction 不足　*fusoku*, insufficiency
29 7 strokes	足				

人 30 2 strokes	ノ 人	NIN, JIN; *hito* [*bito*], person 人類 *jinrui*, human race 人間 *ningen*, human being 人口 *jinkō*, population 亻
子 31 3 strokes	フ 了 子	SHI, SU; *ko* [*go*], child 子ども *kodomo*, child, children 原子 *genshi*, atom 様子 *yōsu*, the state of things, appearance 孑
女 32 3 strokes	〈 女 女	JO, NYO; *onna*, woman, girl 女中 *jochū*, maid 少女 *shōjo*, maiden 女王 *joō*, queen
先 33 6 strokes	ノ ⺊ ⺧ 生 步 先	SEN; *saki*, previous, ahead 先生 *sensei*, teacher 先日 *senjitsu*, the other day 行き先 *yukisaki*, destination
生 34 5 strokes	ノ ⺊ ⺧ 牛 生	SEI, SHŌ; birth, life; *u(mareru)*, to be born; *u(mu)*, to give birth; *i(kiru)*, to live; *ki*, pure, genuine; *nama*, raw 一生 *isshō*, one's (whole) life 生活 *seikatsu*, livelihood 大学生 *daigakusei*, college student

赤	一	十	土	SEKI, SHAKU; *aka*, *aka(i)*, red
	赤	亦	赤	赤ちゃん　*akachan*, baby, infant 赤十字　*sekijūji*, Red Cross 赤銅　*shakudō*, alloy of copper and gold
35 **7 strokes**	赤			

青	一	十	丰	SEI, SHŌ; *ao*, *ao(i)*, blue, green, inexperienced
	主	青	青	青年　*seinen*, youth 青白い　*aojiroi*, pale 青空　*aozora*, blue sky
36 **8 strokes**	青	青		

白	ノ	⺈	白	HAKU, BYAKU; *shiro* [*jiro*], *shiro(i)*, white
	白	白		白人　*hakujin*, Caucasian 白状　*hakujō*, confession 白鳥　*hakuchō*, swan
37 **5 strokes**				

山	丨	山	山	SAN [ZAN]; *yama*, mountain
				山道　*sandō*, *yamamichi*, mountain path 山脈　*sammyaku*, mountain range 登山　*tozan*, mountain climbing
38 **3 strokes**				

川	丿	川	川	SEN; *kawa* [*gawa*], river
				谷川　*tanigawa*, mountain stream 川ばた　*kawabata*, riverside 川口　*kawaguchi*, mouth of a river
39 **3 strokes**				

田 40 5 strokes	丶 ⊓ 田	冂 田	皿	DEN; *ta* [*da*], rice field 田園 *den-en*, fields and gardens, rural districts 稲田 *inada*, rice field 田植 *taue*, rice planting
森 41 12 strokes	一 木 朩	十 朩 森	才 杢 森	SHIN; *mori*, forest, grove 森林 *shinrin*, forest 森閑 *shinkan*, silent 森厳 *shingen*, solemn, awe-inspiring
雨 42 8 strokes	一 帀 雨	冖 雨	冋 雨	U; *ame*, rain 大雨 *ō-ame*, heavy rain 雨戸 *amado*, rain door, shutter 梅雨 *baiu*, rainy season of early summer
花 43 7 strokes	一 艹 花	十 艾	艹 花	KA; *hana*, flower 花屋 *hanaya*, flower shop, florist 花びん *kabin*, vase 花火 *hanabi*, fireworks
石 44 5 strokes	一 石	厂 石	不	SEKI, KOKU, SHAKU; *ishi*, stone 小石 *ko-ishi*, pebble 石炭 *sekitan*, coal 磁石 *jishaku*, magnet

本	一	十	才	**HON [BON, PON]**, book, suffix for counting long, slender objects
	木	本		一本 *ippon*, one (bottle, rod, etc.) 本箱 *hombako*, bookcase 日本 *Nihon, Nippon*, Japan
45 5 strokes				

正	一	丁	下	**SEI, SHŌ**; *tada(shii)*, correct, right
	开	正		正直 *shōjiki*, honesty 正方形 *seihōkei*, square (geometrical figure) 正月 *shōgatsu*, New Year's
46 5 strokes				

雲	一	戸	于	**UN**; *kumo [gumo]*, cloud
	雨	雨	雲	雲状 *unjō*, cloudlike, nebulous 入道雲 *nyūdōgumo*, gigantic clouds
	雪	雲	雲	星雲 *seiun*, nebula (雨 42)
47 12 strokes				

円	丨	冂	冂	**EN**, circle, yen (Japanese monetary unit)
	円			円満 *emman*, perfection, satisfaction ⌈bill 千円札 *sen-ensatsu*, thousand-yen 円盤 *emban*, disc
48 4 strokes				

王	一	丁	干	**Ō**, king
	王			王様 *ōsama*, king 王子 *ōji*, prince 王国 *ōkoku*, kingdom, monarchy
49 4 strokes				王

24

音	丶	亠	立	ON, IN; *ne, oto*, sound
	立	立	产	音楽 *ongaku*, music 発音 *hatsuon*, pronunciation 母音 *boin*, vowel
50 9 strokes	音	音	音	
何	ノ	イ	仁	KA; *nani, (nan)*, what, how many (interrogative prefix)
	仁	何	何	何人 *nannin*, how many people? 何時間 *nanjikan*, how much time? 何時 *nanji*, what time?
51 7 strokes	何			
夏	一	丁	丆	KA; *natsu*, summer
	万	百	百	夏休み *natsuyasumi*, summer vacation 初夏 *shoka*, early summer 真夏 *manatsu*, midsummer
52 10 strokes	夏	夏	夏	(目 25)
家	丶	丶丶	宀	KA, KE; *ya, ie*, house
	宀	宁	宁	家主 *yanushi*, owner of a house, landlord 家族 *kazoku*, family 農家 *nōka*, farmhouse
53 10 strokes	家	家	家	
会	ノ	人	스	KAI, E; meeting; *a(u)*, to meet
	仐	会	会	会場 *kaijō*, place of meeting, site 会長 *kaichō*, president (of a society), chairman (of a committee) 会話 *kaiwa*, conversation
54 6 strokes				

海 55 9 strokes	`	´	⺀ KAI; *umi*, sea, ocean

			KAI; *umi*, sea, ocean
海			海岸　*kaigan*, seacoast, seaside
55 9 strokes			海水浴　*kaisuiyoku*, sea bathing 海外　*kaigai*, overseas, abroad

外 56 5 strokes			GAI, GE (outside, foreign); *hoka*, other; *soto*, outside
			外国　*gaikoku*, foreign country 外国人　*gaikokujin*, foreigner 外科　*geka*, surgery

学 57 8 strokes			GAKU, learning, science; *mana-(bu)*, to learn
			学校　*gakkō*, school 医学　*igaku*, medicine 科学　*kagaku*, science

間 58 12 strokes			KAN, KEN; *aida*, interval, space; *ma*, interval, room, time
			時間　*jikan*, time 二時間　*nijikan*, two hours 昼間　*hiruma*, daytime (⾨ 11)

気 59 6 strokes			KI, KE, spirit, energy, mind
			天気　*tenki*, weather 元気　*genki*, good spirits, health 病気　*byōki*, sickness

26

| 汽 | | | | KI (steam, vapor) |
| 60 7 strokes | | | | 汽車 *kisha*, steam-driven train
汽笛 *kiteki*, steam whistle
汽船 *kisen*, steamship, steamboat |

| 休 | | | | KYŪ; *yasu(mi)*, rest, vacation; *yasu(mu)*, to rest |
| 61 6 strokes | | | | 休憩 *kyūkei*, rest, intermission
休日 *kyūjitsu*, holiday
休養 *kyūyō*, relaxation, recreation |

| 牛 | | | | GYŪ; *ushi*, cow, bull |
| 62 4 strokes | | | | 小牛 *ko-ushi*, calf
牛乳 *gyūnyū*, milk
牛肉 *gyūniku*, beef |

| 京 | | | | KYŌ, capital; KEI |
| 63 8 strokes | | | | 東京 *Tōkyō*, capital of Japan
京都 *Kyōto*, ancient capital of Japan
上京 *jōkyō*, going to Tōkyō |

| 玉 | | | | GYOKU; *tama* [*dama*], jewel, round object |
| 64 5 strokes | | | | 水玉 *mizutama*, drop of water
目玉 *medama*, eyeball |

27

空	丶	宀	宀	KŪ; *sora* [*zora*], sky
	宀	灾	空	青空　*aozora*, blue sky 空気　*kūki*, air 空港　*kūkō*, airport
65 8 strokes	空	空		
犬	一	ナ	大	KEN; *inu*, dog
	犬			小犬　　*ko-inu*, puppy 番犬　　*banken*, watchdog 狂犬病　*kyōkembyō*, rabies
66 4 strokes				
見	丨	冂	月	KEN; *mi(ru)*, to see, to look
	月	目	貝	見せる　*miseru*, to show 見物　　*kembutsu*, sightseeing 見本　　*mihon*, sample
67 7 strokes	見			
元	一	二	テ	GEN, GAN; *moto*, beginning, foundation
	元			根元　*kongen*, root, origin, source 元来　*ganrai*, originally, primarily 元日　*ganjitsu*, New Year's
68 4 strokes				
戸	一	ラ	ョ	KO; *to* [*do*], door
	戸			戸外　*kogai*, outdoors 木戸　*kido*, gate, door 江戸　*Edo*, old name for Tōkyō
69 4 strokes				

古 70 5 strokes	一 十 古 古 古	**KO**; *furu(i)*, old, ancient 古代　*kodai*, ancient times 古今　*kokon*, past and present 考古学　*kōkogaku*, archeology
工 71 3 strokes	一 丁 工	**KŌ, KU** (worker, construction) 工夫　*kōfu*, workman, laborer 工事中　*kōjichū*, under construction 工学　*kōgaku*, engineering
光 72 6 strokes	⟍ ⟍ ⿱ 业 光 光	**KŌ**; *hikari*, light, ray; *hika(ru)*, to shine 光年　*kōnen*, light-year 光波　*kōha*, light wave 観光　*kankō*, sightseeing
行 73 6 strokes	⟍ ⟍ 彳 彳 行 行	**KŌ, GYŌ, AN**; *i(ku)*, *yu(ku)*, to go; *oko(nau)*, to hold, to conduct 行列　*gyōretsu*, procession, queue 急行　*kyūkō*, express 銀行　*ginkō*, bank
考 74 6 strokes	一 十 土 耂 耂 考	**KŌ**; *kanga(e)*, thought, idea, opinion; *kanga(eru)*, to think 参考　*sankō*, reference 考案　*kōan*, idea, plan, scheme 考査　*kōsa*, examination

校	一	十	木	KŌ (school; to correct, to investigate, to compare, to think)
	杧	杧	杧	校正　*kōsei*, proofreading 校舎　*kōsha*, school building
75 **10 strokes**	杦	杦	校	校友　*kōyū*, alumnus (木　15)

高	、	二	古	KŌ; *taka(i)*, high, costly
	产	高	高	高等学校　*kōtōgakkō*, high school 最高　*saikō*, highest 高台　*takadai*, elevated land
76 **10 strokes**				(口　27)

合	ノ	人	入	GŌ; *a(u)*, to be together, to fit
	合	合	合	合図　*aizu*, signal, sign 都合　*tsugō*, circumstances, convenience
77 **6 strokes**				組合　*kumiai*, union

谷	'	ハ	父	KOKU; *tani*, valley
	父	谷	谷	谷間　*tanima*, valley 谷底　*tanizoko*, bottom of a ravine
78 **7 strokes**	谷			

国	丨	冂	冋	KOKU; *kuni* [*guni*], country
	冃	囯	国	国語　*kokugo*, national language (Japanese) 国会　*kokkai*, the National Diet
79 **8 strokes**	国	国		全国　*zenkoku*, national

黒 80 11 strokes	丶	冂	日	KOKU; *kuro* [*guro*], *kuro(i)*, black 黒人　*kokujin*, negro 黒板　*kokuban*, blackboard 暗黒　*ankoku*, darkness, blackness
	甲	里	里	
	里	黒	黒	

| 今 81 4 strokes | 丿 | 人 | 𠆢 | KON, KIN; *ima*, now, the present

今月　*kongetsu*, this month
今度　*kondo*, next time
今夜　*kon-ya*, tonight |
| | 今 | | | |

作 82 7 strokes	丿	亻	𠂉	SAKU, SA; *tsuku(ru)*, to make 作文　*sakubun*, (literary) composition 名作　*meisaku*, masterpiece 作曲　*sakkyoku*, musical composition
	伬	佧	作	
	作			

| 糸 83 6 strokes | く | 幺 | 幺 | SHI; *ito*, thread

毛糸　*keito*, woolen yarn
糸口　*itoguchi*, clue
糸巻　*itomaki*, spool for thread |
| | 糸 | 糸 | 糸 | |

思 84 9 strokes	丶	冂	冊	SHI; *omo(u)*, to think, to recall 思想　*shisō*, thought, idea 不思議　*fushigi*, strange 思い出　*omoide*, remembrance, recollection
	田	田	田	
	思	思	思	

31

紙	幺	幺	糸
	糸	糸	糸
85 10 strokes	紅	紙	紙

SHI; *kami* [*gami*], paper

ボール紙　*bōrugami*, cardboard
表紙　　　*hyōshi*, cover, binding
紙くず　　*kamikuzu*, wastepaper

(糸 83)

字	丶	丷	宀
	宀	宁	字
86 6 strokes			

JI, letter, mark; *aza*, section (of a village)

字引　*jibiki*, dictionary
文字　*monji*, *moji*, letter, character, ideograph
数字　*sūji*, number, numeral

時	丨	冂	日
	日一	日十	昨
87 10 strokes	眭	時	時

JI; *toki* [*doki*], time

時々　*tokidoki*, sometimes
時計　*tokei*, watch, clock
時代　*jidai*, period, epoch

車	一	匚	冋
	写	百	亘
88 7 strokes	車		

SHA; *kuruma* [*guruma*], wheel, vehicle

自動車　*jidōsha*, automobile
自転車　*jitensha*, bicycle
発車　　*hassha*, departure of a vehicle

秋	丿	二	千
	禾	禾	禾
89 9 strokes	秋	秋	秋

SHŪ; *aki*, fall, autumn

初秋　*shoshū*, early autumn
秋風　*akikaze*, autumn breeze
秋分　*shūbun*, autumnal equinox

| 出 90 5 strokes | 丨 | 屮 | 屮 | SHUTSU, SUI; de(ru), to come out, to go out; da(su), to put out, to take out, to bring out, to draw out |
| | 出 | 出 | | 出発 shuppatsu, setting out, departure, starting
出版 shuppan, publishing
出口 deguchi, exit |

春 91 9 strokes	一	二	三	SHUN; haru, spring
	丰	夫	夫	春風 harukaze, spring breeze 青春 seishun, springtime of life 晩春 banshun, late spring
	春	春	春	

書 92 10 strokes	ㄱ	ㅋ	ㅋ	SHO; ka(ku), to write
	ㅋ	彐	聿	辞書 jisho, dictionary 書物 shomotsu, book, volume 教科書 kyōkasho, textbook
	書	書	書	

| 少 93 4 strokes | 丿 | 川 | 小 | SHŌ; suko(shi), suku(nai), few, little, scarce |
| | 少 | | | 少年 shōnen, boy, lad ⌈what
多少 tashō, more or less, some-
少佐 shōsa, major (army), lieutenant commander (navy) |

| 色 94 6 strokes | 丿 | ク | 夕 | SHIKI, SHOKU; iro, color |
| | 名 | 名 | 色 | 顔色 kao-iro, complexion
天然色 tennenshoku, natural color, technicolor
色彩 shikisai, color, hue |

心 95 4 strokes	㇔ 心	心	心	**SHIN**; *kokoro* [*gokoro*], spirit, heart, mind 心持ち *kokoromochi*, mood, feeling, sensation 「tion 真心 *magokoro*, sincerity, devo- 一心 *isshin*, whole-heartedness
西 96 6 strokes	一 両	厂 西	西 西	**SEI, SAI**; *nishi*, west 西洋 *seiyō*, the West, the Occident 大西洋 *Taiseiyō*, Atlantic Ocean 東西 *tōzai*, east and west, Orient and Occident
声 97 7 strokes	一 吉 声	十 声	士 声	**SEI**; *koe* [*goe*], voice 泣き声 *nakigoe*, crying voice 音声学 *onseigaku*, phonetics 声帯 *seitai*, the vocal cords
夕 98 3 strokes	ノ	ク	夕	**SEKI**; *yū*, evening 夕方 *yūgata*, evening 夕飯 *yūhan*, supper 夕風 *yūkaze*, evening breeze
切 99 4 strokes	一 切	七	切	**SETSU, SAI**; *ki(ru)*, to cut 一切れ *hitokire*, one slice 親切 *shinsetsu*, kindness 一切 *issai*, all, everything

雪	一	厂	戸	SETSU; *yuki*, snow
	雨	雨	雨	雪だるま *yukidaruma*, snowman 雪解け *yukidoke*, thaw 積雪 *sekisetsu*, snowdrift
100 11 strokes	雪	雪	雪	(雨 42)

千	ノ	二	千	SEN [ZEN], *chi*, thousand
				千円 *sen-en*, a thousand yen 三千 *sanzen*, three thousand 五千 *gosen*, five thousand
101 3 strokes				

前	丶	丷	丷	ZEN; *mae*, before, in front of, previous
	亠	竹	前	午前 *gozen*, morning, A.M. 前後 *zengo*, before and after, context
102 9 strokes	前	前	前	以前 *izen*, ago, since, before

組	く	幺	幺	SO; *kumi* [*gumi*], class, group, set; *ku(mu)*, to join, to unite
	糸	糹	糺	組み立て *kumitate*, construction, structure 「class 一組 *hitokumi*, one set, one
103 11 strokes	糺	組	組	番組 *bangumi*, program (糸 83)

早	丶	口	日	SŌ; *haya* [*baya*], *haya(i)*, early, fast
	日	旦	早	早口 *haya-guchi*, quick speaking
104 6 strokes				早春 *sōshun*, early spring 手早い *tebayai*, quick, nimble

走	一	十	土	SŌ; *hashi(ru)*, to run
	丰	丰	赱	競走 *kyōsō*, race, running match
105 7 strokes	走			走り書き *hashirigaki*, hasty writing 走り去る *hashirisaru*, to run away
草	一	十	艹	SŌ; *kusa [gusa]*, grass, vegetation
	艹	芏	苩	草原 *kusahara (kusawara)*, grassy plain 草案 *sōan*, draft (of a manuscript)
106 9 strokes	苩	苩	草	草取り *kusatori*, weeding
村	一	十	才	SON; *mura*, village
	木	村	村	村民 *sommin*, villager 村長 *sonchō*, village mayor 農村 *nōson*, a farm village
107 7 strokes	村			
多	ノ	ク	タ	TA; *ō(i)*, many, much, abundant
	夕	多	多	多数 *tasū*, large number 多分 *tabun*, perhaps 多量 *taryō*, great quantity
108 6 strokes				
男	丶	冂	冊	DAN, NAN; *otoko*, man, male
	冊	田	男	男性 *dansei*, male sex, male 男子 *danshi*, male, boy 長男 *chōnan*, eldest son
109 7 strokes	男			

池

110
6 strokes

CHI; *ike*, pond, lake

電池	*denchi*, electric cell, battery
池畔	*chihan*, side of a pond, around a pond
用水池	*yōsuichi*, reservoir

地

111
6 strokes

CHI, JI, earth, ground

地上	*chijō*, on the ground
地下	*chika*, underground
地面	*jimen*, surface of the earth

知

112
8 strokes

CHI; *shi*(*ru*), to know; *shi*(*raseru*), to inform

知識	*chishiki*, knowledge
知人	*chijin*, an acquaintance
承知	*shōchi*, assent, agreement

竹

113
6 strokes

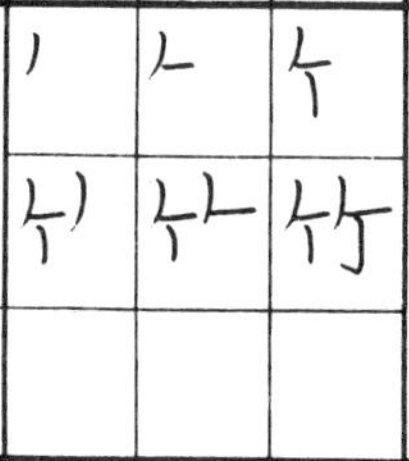

CHIKU; *take* [*dake*], bamboo

竹やぶ	*takeyabu*, bamboo grove
竹細工	*takezaiku*, bamboo ware
竹かご	*takekago*, bamboo basket

虫

114
6 strokes

CHŪ; *mushi*, insect, bug, worm

害虫	*gaichū*, harmful insect
虫歯	*mushiba*, decayed tooth
こん虫	*konchū*, insect, bug

町	丶	冂	冂	CHŌ; *machi*, town
	冊	田	田	町はずれ *machihazure*, outskirts of a town
115 7 strokes	町			町内 *chōnai*, the neighborhood
				町長 *chōchō*, mayor of a town

長	丶	匚	F	CHŌ, head of an institution or organization; *naga(i)*, long
	F	圧	長	細長い *hosonagai*, long and narrow
116 8 strokes	長	長		長ぐつ *nagagutsu*, boots
				校長 *kōchō*, principal of a school

鳥	丶	亻	宀	CHŌ; *tori* [*dori*], bird
	白	鳥	鳥	鳥類 *chōrui*, birds (as a species)
117 11 strokes	鳥	鳥	鳥	小鳥 *kotori*, small bird
				渡り鳥 *wataridori*, migratory bird

朝	一	十	十	CHŌ; *asa*, morning
	古	古	卣	朝刊 *chōkan*, morning paper
118 12 strokes	直	卓	朝	朝食 *chōshoku*, breakfast
				毎朝 *mai-asa*, every morning
				(月 12)

天	一	二	于	TEN, *ame*, sky, heaven
	天			天気 *tenki*, weather
119 4 strokes				天井 *tenjō*, ceiling
				天才 *tensai*, genius

38

冬 120 5 strokes	ノ	ク	夂	TŌ; *fuyu*, winter
	冬	冬		冬休み *fuyuyasumi*, winter vacation
				冬眠 *tōmin*, hibernation
				冬期 *tōki*, winter season

東 121 8 strokes	一	厂	亓	TŌ; *higashi*, east
	币	百	東	東側 *higashigawa*, east side
	東	東		東洋 *tōyō*, the East, the Orient
				北東 *hokutō*, northeast

道 122 12 strokes	丶	丷	丷	DŌ; *michi*, road, path
	丷	首	首	水道 *suidō*, waterworks
	丷首	道	道	道具 *dōgu*, tool
				鉄道 *tetsudō*, railroad
				(日 25)

読 123 14 strokes	丶	二	言	DOKU, TOKU; *yo(mu)*, to read
	言	計	詰	読者 *dokusha*, reader (person)
	詩	読	読	読書 *dokusho*, reading
				読み返す *yomikaesu*, to reread
				(口 27, 士 410)

南 124 9 strokes	一	十	十	NAN; *minami*, south
	南	南	南	南部 *nambu*, southern part
	南	南	南	南極 *Nankyoku*, South Pole
				西南 *seinan*, southwest

入	ノ	入		NYŪ; *iri*, entering, attendance; *i(reru)*, to put in 入学 *nyūgaku*, entering school 輸入 *yunyū*, importation 入口 *iriguchi*, entrance
125 **2 strokes**				

年	ノ	⌐	⌐	NEN; *toshi*, year 六年生 *rokunensei*, sixth-grade pupil 年寄り *toshiyori*, old person 青年 *seinen*, youth
	仁	仁	年	
126 **6 strokes**				

馬	丨	厂	𠃌	BA; *uma*, horse 馬車 *basha*, carriage 競馬場 *keibajō*, race track
	厍	馬	馬	
	馬	馬	馬	
127 **10 strokes**				

麦	一	十	主	BAKU; *mugi*, barley, wheat 麦わら *mugiwara*, (barley) straw 麦刈り *mugikari*, mowing barley 小麦 *komugi*, wheat
	主	寿	寿	
	麦			
128 **7 strokes**				

半	丶	丷	丷	HAN; *naka(ba)*, half 半分 *hambun*, half 一時半 *ichiji-han*, one-thirty, half-past one 半島 *hantō*, peninsula
	半	半		
129 **5 strokes**				

百	一	二	丂	HYAKU [BYAKU], hundred
	万	百	百	二百　*nihyaku*, two hundred 三百　*sambyaku*, three hundred 百貨店　*hyakkaten*, department store
130 6 strokes				

父	ノ	ハ	分	FU; *chichi*, father
	父			父兄会　*fukeikai*, parents' association 祖父　*sofu*, grandfather 父母　*fubo*, parents
131 4 strokes				

風	ノ	几	凡	FŪ; *kaze*, wind
	凡	凬	凨	風景　*fūkei*, scenery 台風　*taifū*, typhoon 南風　*minamikaze*, south wind
132 9 strokes	風	風	風	

分	ノ	ハ	分	FUN [PUN], minute; BUN, BU, part, share; *wa(keru)*, to divide, to separate (v.t.); *wa(kareru)*, to be divided, to branch off
	分			自分　*jibun*, self 二分　*nifun*, two minutes 十分　*jippun*, ten minutes
133 4 strokes				

文	、	亠	方	BUN, writings, a sentence; MON, ancient unit of money
	文			文化　*bunka*, culture 文学　*bungaku*, literature 文部省　*Mombushō*, Ministry of Education
134 4 strokes				

米 135 6 strokes	ヽ 半	ヽ 米	丷 米	**BEI** (America, rice), **MAI** (rice); *kome*, rice 米国　*Beikoku*, America, the United States 米作　*beisaku*, rice-growing (crop) 白米　*hakumai*, polished rice
歩 136 8 strokes	⌁ 止 歩	⌐ 눠 歩	止 步	**HO** [**PO**], **BU**; *ayu(mu)*, *aru(ku)*, to walk, to step 第一歩　*dai-ippo*, the first step 進歩　*shimpo*, progress 散歩　*sampo*, a walk, a stroll
母 137 5 strokes	𠃋 囚	⺄ 母	刄 母	**BO**; *haha*, mother 母の日　*Haha-no-hi*, Mother's Day 母国　*bokoku*, mother country 母親　*haha-oya*, mother
方 138 4 strokes	ヽ 方	亠	方	**HŌ** [**PŌ**], direction, side; *kata* [*gata*], side, way of ~ing, person 両方　*ryōhō*, both sides 作り方　*tsukurikata*, way of making 夕方　*yūgata*, evening
北 139 5 strokes	一 北	十 北	土	**HOKU** [**BOKU**]; *kita*, north 北極　*Hokkyoku*, North Pole 南北　*namboku*, north and south 北風　*kitakaze*, north wind

42

名 140 6 strokes	ノ ク タ タ 名 名	MEI, MYŌ (name, fame); *na*, name 名まえ　*namae*, name 有名　*yūmei*, famous, well-known 名人　*meijin*, an expert
明 141 8 strokes	l 冂 日 日 日) 明 明 明	MEI, MYŌ (bright); *aka(rui)*, light, bright; *aki(raka)*, bright; *a(keru)*, to dawn, to break (day) 夜明け　*yoake*, dawn 説明　*setsumei*, explanation 発明　*hatsumei*, invention
毛 142 4 strokes	ノ 二 三 毛	MŌ; *ke*, hair 毛糸　*keito*, woolen thread, yarn 毛虫　*kemushi*, caterpillar 毛布　*mōfu*, blanket
門 143 8 strokes	l 冂 尸 尸 尸 門 門 門	MON, gate; *kado*, gate 校門　*kōmon*, school gate 専門　*semmon*, specialty 門口　*kadoguchi*, door, entrance
夜 144 8 strokes	` 一 广 广 亦 夜 夜 夜	YA; *yo*, *yoru*, evening, night 夜中　*yonaka*, midnight 十五夜　*jūgoya*, night of the full moon 今夜　*kon-ya*, tonight

| 友 | 一 ナ 友 友 | YŪ; *tomo*, friend

友だち *tomodachi*, friend
友人 *yūjin*, friend
友情 *yūjō*, friendship |
| 145
4 strokes | | |

| 用 | 丿 冂 月 月 用 | YŌ, business; *mochi(iru)*, to use

用意 *yōi*, preparation
用心 *yōjin*, heed, care, caution
用事 *yōji*, business |
| 146
5 strokes | | |

| 来 | 一 ⼀ ⼀ 立 平 来 来 | RAI; *ku(ru)*, to come; *ki(masu)*, come (present tense); *ko(i)*, come (imperative)

来年 *rainen*, next year
以来 *irai*, since, from that time
将来 *shōrai*, the future |
| 147
7 strokes | | |

| 力 | ㇆ 力 | RIKI, RYOKU; *chikara*, strength, power

力持 *chikaramochi*, strong person
協力 *kyōryoku*, co-operation
努力 *doryoku*, endeavor |
| 148
2 strokes | | |

| 立 | 丶 亠 六 立 立 | RITSU; *ta(tsu)*, *tachi* [*dachi*], to stand

独立 *dokuritsu*, independence
役立つ *yakudatsu*, useful
立場 *tachiba*, standpoint |
| 149
5 strokes | | |

44

林

150
8 strokes

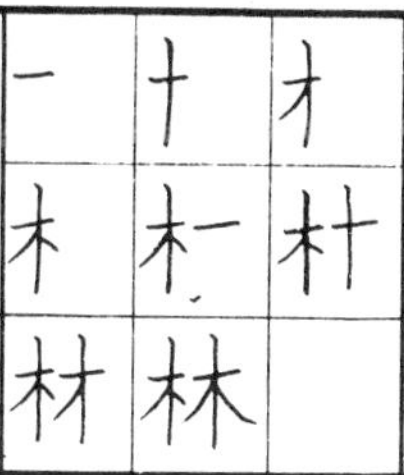

RIN; *hayashi* [*bayashi*], woods

植林 *shokurin*, reforestation
密林 *mitsurin*, thick forest
農林 *nōrin*, agriculture and forestry

話

151
13 strokes

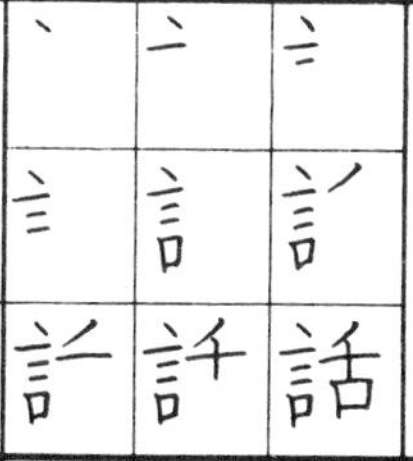

WA; *hanashi* [*banashi*], story; *hana(su)*, to speak

世話 *sewa*, aid
電話 *denwa*, telephone
会話 *kaiwa*, conversation

(口 27)

悪

152
11 strokes

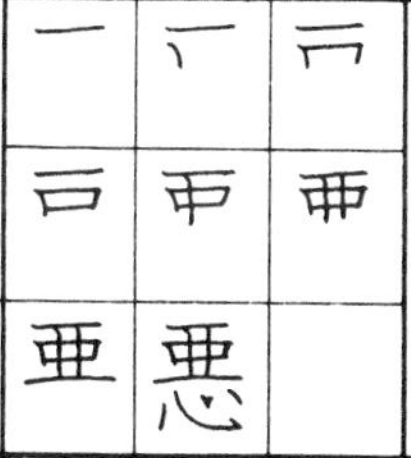

AKU, badness, evil; *waru(i)*, bad, evil

悪口 *warukuchi*, evil talk, gossip
悪人 *akunin*, bad man, villain
悪路 *akuro*, bad road

(心 95)

安

153
6 strokes

AN; *yasu(i)*, cheap, inexpensive

安心 *anshin*, peace of mind
安全 *anzen*, safe
不安 *fuan*, uneasiness

暗

154
13 strokes

AN; *kura(i)*, dark

まっ暗 *makkura*, pitch dark
暗号 *angō*, code, cryptograph
暗記 *anki*, memorization

(音 50)

意 155 13 strokes	丶 立 音 音	亠 产 音 音	立 音 意	I, mind, heart, attention, care

I, mind, heart, attention, care

注意　*chūi*, care, attention
意見　*iken*, opinion, admonition
意味　*imi*, meaning

(立 149, 心 95)

引 156 4 strokes	⁊ 引	⁊	弓	IN; *hiki* [*biki*], pulling; *hi(ku)*, to pull, to draw

IN; *hiki* [*biki*], pulling; *hi(ku)*, to pull, to draw

福引き　*fukubiki*, lottery
引用　*in-yō*, quotation, citation
引き立て　*hikitate*, favor, patronage

運 157 12 strokes	冒 軍	⊓ 宣 渾	⊓ 軍 運	UN, luck; *hako(bu)*, to carry, to transport

UN, luck; *hako(bu)*, to carry, to transport

運よく　*un-yoku*, luckily
運動　*undō*, exercise, motion
運命　*ummei*, fate

(車 88)

駅 158 14 strokes	丨 馬 馬⁊	厂 馬 駅⁊	厅 馬⁊ 駅	EKI, station

EKI, station

駅前　*ekimae*, in front of the station
駅長　*ekichō*, station master
駅員　*eki-in*, station employee

(馬 127)

園 159 13 strokes	丿 肙 肙	⊓ 肙 園	冂 肙 園	EN; *sono* [*zono*], garden

EN; *sono* [*zono*], garden

公園　*kōen*, public park
花園　*hanazono*, flower garden
動物園　*dōbutsu-en*, zoo

(土 17, 口 27)

遠	土	吉	青	EN, ON; *tō(i)*, far, distant
	青	素	袁	遠足　*ensoku*, excursion, long walk 遠方　*empō*, long distance 永遠　*eien*, eternity
160 13 strokes	遠	遠	遠	(土 17, 口 27)

屋	ㄱ	コ	尸	OKU; *ya*, shop
	尸	尼	层	屋根　　*yane*, roof 時計屋　*tokeiya*, watch shop 屋上　　*okujō*, housetop, roof
161 9 strokes	居	屋	屋	

温	氵	氵	沪	ON (warm)
	沪	沪	沪	温度　*ondo*, temperature 温泉　*onsen*, hot spring 体温　*taion*, body temperature
162 12 strokes	渦	渦	温	(氵 汽 60)

化	ノ	イ	イ	KA, KE; *ba(keru)*, to take the form of; *ba(kasu)*, to bewitch
	化			変化　*henka*, change, variation, alteration
163 4 strokes				化学　*kagaku*, chemistry 化粧　*keshō*, make-up

科	ノ	二	千	KA, course, branch
	千	禾	禾	学科　　*gakka*, a school subject 教科書　*kyōkasho*, textbook 科学　　*kagaku*, science
164 9 strokes	禾	科	科	

47

荷 165 10 strokes	一 艹 艾 艾 艾 荷 荷 荷 荷	KA; *ni*, a load, burden 荷物　*nimotsu*, baggage 荷船　*nibune*, freighter 荷作り　*nizukuri*, packing
歌 166 14 strokes	一 可 可 哥 哥 哥 歌 歌 歌	KA; *uta*, song; *uta(u)*, to sing 国歌　*kokka*, national anthem 歌劇　*kageki*, opera 歌手　*kashu*, singer (口　27)
画 167 8 strokes	一 丆 亓 币 雨 面 画 画	GA (a picture); KAKU, stroke (of a Japanese character) 図画　*zuga*, a drawing 映画　*eiga*, moving picture 計画　*keikaku*, plan
回 168 6 strokes	丨 冂 冋 同 回 回	KAI, a turn; *mawa(su)*, to turn (v.t.); *mawa(ru)*, to turn (v.i.) 何回　*nankai*, how many times? 回転　*kaiten*, revolution, rotation 回数　*kaisū*, number of times, frequency
貝 169 7 strokes	丨 冂 月 月 目 貝 貝	*kai* [*gai*], sea shell 貝がら　*kaigara*, shell 貝拾い　*kaihiroi*, shell gathering 真珠貝　*shinjugai*, pearl oyster

48

界	丶	冂	冊	KAI (world)
	田	田	界	世界　　*sekai*, world 世界一　*sekai-ichi*, best in the world
170 9 strokes	界	界	界	限界　　*genkai*, boundary, limits

開	尸	尸	尸	KAI; *hira(ku)*, to open (v. t. & i.)
	門	門	門	開会　　*kaikai*, opening a meeting 満開　　*mankai*, full bloom 開発　　*kaihatsu*, development, exploitation
171 12 strokes	閂	開	開	(門　143)

絵	乚	幺	糸	KAI; E, picture
	糸	糾	給	浮世絵　*ukiyoe*, Japanese print 絵葉書　*ehagaki*, picture postcard さし絵　*sashie*, illustration
172 12 strokes	絵	絵	絵	(糸　83)

角	丿	ク	冂	KAKU, angle; *tsuno*, horn (of an animal)
	角	角	角	三角　　*sankaku*, triangle 四角　　*shikaku*, square 角度　　*kakudo*, angle
173 7 strokes	角			

活	丶	丷	氵	KATSU (energy)
	氵	汁	汗	生活　　*seikatsu*, life 活動　　*katsudō*, activity 活字　　*katsuji*, printer's type
174 9 strokes	汗	活	活	

49

寒	宀	宀	宀	KAN, the coldest season of the year; *samu(i)*, cold
	宀	宙	宲	極寒 *gokkan*, bitter cold 寒中 *kanchū*, cold season 寒流 *kanryū*, cold current
175 12 strokes	寒	寒	寒	

感	ノ	厂	厂	KAN, feeling, thought
	后	咸	咸	感想 *kansō*, thoughts, impressions 感心 *kanshin*, admiration 感覚 *kankaku*, sensation
176 13 strokes	咸	感		(心 95, 口 27)

岸	ノ	屮	山	GAN; *kishi* [*gishi*], bank, shore
	屮	屵	屵	海岸 *kaigan*, seashore 岸壁 *gampeki*, quay, wharf 川岸 *kawagishi*, riverbank
177 8 strokes	岸	岸		

岩	ノ	屮	山	GAN; *iwa*, rock, crag
	屮	屵	岩	花こう岩 *kakōgan*, granite 岩石 *ganseki*, rock 岩屋 *iwaya*, cavern
178 8 strokes	岩	岩		

顔	立	产	彦	GAN; *kao*, face
	彦	彦	彦	顔面 *gammen*, face 顔色 *kao-iro*, complexion 顔付 *kaotsuki*, face, look, countenance
179 18 strokes	彦	彦	顔	(立 149, 貝 169)

記 180 10 strokes	ヽ 言 訂	二 言 記	ニ 訂	**KI** (chronicle) 日記 *nikki*, diary 記念 *kinen*, remembrance, souvenir 記者 *kisha*, journalist (口 27)

起 181 10 strokes	土 赱 起	走 走	走 起	**KI**; *o(kiru)*, to rise, to get up; *o(kosu)*, to raise, to awaken (v.t.) 早起き *hayaoki*, early rising 起原 *kigen*, origin 起重機 *kijūki*, crane, derrick (土 17)

帰 182 10 strokes	ー リヨ 帰	リ リヨ 帰	リ 帰	**KI**; *kae(ru)*, to return, to leave 帰り道 *kaerimichi*, (on) one's way back 帰化人 *kikajin*, naturalized person 帰国 *kikoku*, return to one's native country

期 183 12 strokes	一 廿 其	十 甘 其	廿 甚 期	**KI, GO** (period, term) 学期 *gakki*, school term 期待 *kitai*, expectation 時期 *jiki*, the times, season (月 12)

客 184 9 strokes	ヽ 宀 客	ハ 宊 客	宀 灾 客	**KYAKU, KAKU**, guest お客さん *o-kyaku-san*, guest 客車 *kyakusha*, railroad passenger car 客船 *kyakusen*, passenger boat

究	`丶`	`丷`	`宀`	KYŪ (study)
	`宀`	`灾`	`究`	研究　　　*kenkyū*, research 研究会　*kenkyūkai*, research society 研究家　*kenkyūka*, researcher
185 7 strokes	`究`			

急	`丿`	`勹`	`夕`	KYŪ; *iso(gu)*, to hurry
	`刍`	`刍`	`急`	急病　　*kyūbyō*, sudden illness 急行　　*kyūkō*, express 大急ぎ　*ō-isogi*, great haste
186 9 strokes	`急`	`急`	`急`	

級	`く`	`纟`	`幺`	KYŪ, rank, grade
	`糸`	`糸`	`糸`	学級　　　*gakkyū*, school class 上級　　　*jōkyū*, high class 同級生　*dōkyūsei*, classmate
187 9 strokes	`紀`	`級`	`級`	

球	`丁`	`王`	`王`	KYŪ, sphere, globe
	`珏`	`珏`	`珏`	野球　*yakyū*, baseball 地球　*chikyū*, the earth, the globe 電球　*denkyū*, electric light bulb
188 11 strokes	`球`	`球`	`球`	(E. 49)

去	`一`	`十`	`土`	KYO, KO (past); *sa(ru)*, to leave, to depart
	`去`	`去`		去年　*kyonen*, last year 過去　*kako*, the past, past tense
189 5 strokes				

魚	ノ	ク	⼍	GYO; *uo*, fish
	名	角	角	金魚　　*kingyo*, goldfish 魚市場　*uo-ichiba*, fish market 魚つり　*uotsuri*, fishing
190 11 strokes	角	魚	魚	(灬 点 285)

教	土	耂	耂	KYŌ; *oshi(eru)*, to teach
	孝	孝	孝	教室　*kyōshitsu*, classroom 教育　*kyōiku*, education 教会　*kyōkai*, church
191 11 strokes	教	教	教	(土 17)

強	⼸	コ	弓	KYŌ, GŌ; *tsuyo(i)*, strong
	弘	弘	弘	勉強　*benkyō*, study 強弱　*kyōjaku*, strength and weakness 強情　*gōjō*, obstinacy
192 11 strokes	強	強	強	(虫 114)

橋	木	杧	杧	KYŌ; *hashi* [*bashi*], bridge
	杬	柙	梌	さん橋　*sambashi*, pier 土橋　*dobashi*, earthen bridge 鉄橋　*tekkyō*, iron bridge
193 16 strokes	橋	橋	橋	(木 15, 冂 27)

局	コ	⼮	尸	KYOKU, bureau, board, office, department
	弓	局	局	放送局　*hōsōkyoku*, broadcasting station 編集局　*henshūkyoku*, editorial department 郵便局　*yūbinkyoku*, post office
194 7 strokes	局			

近	ノ	イ	←	**KIN**; *chika(i)*, near
	斤	沂	沂	近道 *chikamichi*, shortcut 近所 *kinjo*, neighborhood 最近 *saikin*, recently
195 7 strokes	近			

銀	ハ	乍	金	**GIN**, silver
	金ヿ	釒ヨ	釒ヨ	銀行 *ginkō*, bank 銀色 *gin-iro*, silver color 銀貨 *ginka*, silver coin
196 14 strokes	鈤	銀	銀	(金 16)

苦	一	十	ㅛ	**KU**, pain, anxiety; *kuru(shii)*, painful; *niga(i)*, bitter
	丱	芢	苦	苦労 *kurō*, troubles, toil 苦心 *kushin*, pains, hard work 苦戦 *kusen*, hard fighting
197 8 strokes	苦	苦		

君	フ	ㅋ	ヨ	**KUN**, Mister, Master; *kimi*, you (familiar form)
	尹	尹	君	佐藤君 *Satō-kun*, Mr. Satō 貴君 *kikun*, you (lit., masc.) 諸君 *shokun*, gentlemen, ladies and gentlemen, you
198 7 strokes	君			

兄	丶	口	口	**KEI**, **KYŌ**; *ani*, older brother
		尸	兄	兄弟 *kyōdai*, brothers (and sisters) 父兄 *fukei*, guardians (of pupils)
199 5 strokes				

形 200 7 strokes	一 二 于 开 开′ 形 形	KEI, GYŌ; *katachi*, ~*gata*, shape, form 人形　　*ningyō*, doll 長方形　*chōhōkei*, rectangle 半円形　*han-enkei*, semicircle
計 201 9 strokes	丶 ニ 亠 言 言 言 言 計 計	KEI; *haka(ru)*, to measure 合計　　*gōkei*, sum, total 寒暖計　*kandankei*, weather thermometer 体温計　*taionkei*, clinical thermometer
決 202 7 strokes	丶 冫 冫 氵 江 決 決	KETSU; *ki(maru)*, to be decided; *ki(meru)*, to decide 決心　*kesshin*, making up one's mind 決定　*kettei*, decision 解決　*kaiketsu*, solution
県 203 9 strokes	丨 冂 月 月 目 且 県 県 県	KEN, prefecture 県道　　*kendō*, prefectural road 県庁　　*kenchō*, prefectural office 県知事　*kenchiji*, prefectural governor
研 204 9 strokes	一 厂 ナ 石 石 石 石 研 研	KEN (study) 研究　　*kenkyū*, study, research 研究室　*kenkyūshitsu*, laboratory 研究所　*kenkyūjo*, research institute

原	一	厂	厂	GEN (original); *hara* (*wara*), field, meadow
	厃	厏	原	原因　*gen-in*, cause
				高原　*kōgen*, plateau
205 10 strokes	原	原	原	草原　*kusawara*, grassy plain (小 24)

庫	`	一	广	KO (warehouse)
	广	庐	庐	書庫　*shoko*, library 倉庫　*sōko*, warehouse
				冷蔵庫　*reizōko*, icebox, refrigerator
206 10 strokes	庐	庫	庫	(車 88)

午	ノ	一	午	GO (noon)
	午			午前　*gozen*, morning, A.M. 午後　*gogo*, afternoon, P.M. 正午　*shōgo*, noon
207 4 strokes				

後	`	ク	彳	GO, KŌ; *ushi*(*ro*), behind; *nochi*, after
	徉	往	徔	食後　*shokugo*, after a meal 最後　*saigo*, last
	移	務	後	前後　*zengo*, before and after, context
208 9 strokes				

語	`	二	言	GO, word, speech; *katari* [*gatari*], narration; *kata*(*ru*), to tell, to speak
	言	訁	訂	外国語　*gaikokugo*, foreign language
	訝	語	語	英語　*eigo*, English language 物語　*monogatari*, tale
209 14 strokes				(II 27)

公 210 4 strokes	ノ 公	八	公	KŌ; *ōyake*, public 主人公　*shujinkō*, hero, heroine 公園　*kōen*, public park 公転　*kōten*, revolution, turning
広 211 5 strokes	丶 広	亠 広	广	KŌ; *hiro(i)*, wide; *hiro(geru)*, to spread (v.t.); *hiro(garu)*, to spread (v.i.); *hiro(maru)*, to be spread 広場　*hiroba*, open space, plaza 広告　*kōkoku*, advertisement 広大　*kōdai*, vast
交 212 6 strokes	丶 六	亠 亥	六 交	KŌ; *ma(jiru)*, to be mixed; *maji-(waru)*, to associate with 交際　*kōsai*, intercourse, associa-tion 交番　*kōban*, police box 交通　*kōtsū*, traffic
向 213 6 strokes	ノ 向	亻 向	勹 向	KŌ; *mu(ku)*, to turn toward, to be suited for; *mu(kau)*, to face, to head for 向こう　*mukō*, opposite 向こう側　*mukōgawa*, opposite side 方向　*hōkō*, direction, course
黄 214 11 strokes	一 荊 黃	艹 芇 菄	圦 带 黄	KŌ, Ō; *ki*, yellow 黄色　*ki-iro*, yellow 黄金　*ōgon*, gold 黄熱病　*ōnetsubyō*, yellow fever (艹 草 106)

号	ヽ 口 口	GŌ, number, issue (of a magazine)
	므 号	番号 *bangō*, number 記号 *kigō*, symbol 信号 *shingō*, signal, code
215 5 strokes		

根	一 十 木	KON, root (math.), perseverance; *ne*, root
	村 村 柯	根気 *konki*, patience, perseverance 大根 *daikon*, giant white radish
216 10 strokes	柠 根 根	根本 *kompon*, basis

才	一 十 才	SAI, talent, suffix for counting age
		十六才 *jūroku-sai*, sixteen years old 天才 *tensai*, genius
217 3 strokes		才能 *sainō*, talent

細	く 纟 幺	SAI; *hoso(i)*, slender, narrow; *ko-ma(kai)*, minute, fine, detailed
	糸 糾 紀	細道 *hosomichi*, narrow road 細工 *saiku*, work, craftsmanship
218 11 strokes	細 細 細	細菌 *saikin*, bacillus, germ (糸 83)

算	ノ ㇄ ㇰ	SAN [ZAN] (reckoning)
	ㄥㄥ ㄥㄥ 管	算数 *sansū*, arithmetic, calculation 計算 *keisan*, computation, figuring
219 14 strokes	筧 算 算	予算 *yosan*, budget (目 25)

止	丨	卜	止	SHI; *to(maru)*, to stop (v.i.); *to-(meru)*, to bring to a stop; *tome* [*dome*], stop
	止			中止 *chūshi*, discontinuation 禁止 *kinshi*, prohibition 通行止 *tsūkōdome*, suspension of traffic
220 4 strokes				

仕	ノ	亻	仁	SHI (work); *tsuka(eru)*, to serve
	什	仕		仕事 *shigoto*, work 給仕 *kyūji*, office boy, waiter 仕方 *shikata*, way of doing
221 5 strokes				

市	丶	亠	广	SHI, city; *ichi*, market
	方	市		市役所 *shiyakusho*, city office 市場 *ichiba*, *shijō*, market 都市 *toshi*, cities
222 5 strokes				

死	一	厂	歹	SHI, death; *shi(nu)*, to die
	歹	歹	死	死体 *shitai*, corpse 死傷者 *shishōsha*, dead and injured, casualties 必死 *hisshi*, certain death, desperation
223 6 strokes				

使	ノ	亻	仁	SHI; *tsuka(u)*, to use
	仁	侣	佢	使い *tsukai*, errand, messenger 使命 *shimei*, mission, errand 使用 *shiyō*, use
224 8 strokes	伊	使		

始	く	ㄠ	文	SHI; *haji(maru)*, to begin (v.i.); *haji(meru)*, to begin (v.t.)
	女	女	女	開始 *kaishi*, commencement, start 始末 *shimatsu*, circumstances, the particulars; management
225 8 strokes	始	始		始業 *shigyō*, beginning of work or class

指	一	十	扌	SHI; *yubi*, finger
	扩	拤	扗	親指 *oyayubi*, thumb 指輪 *yubiwa*, ring 指揮者 *shikisha*, conductor, commander
226 9 strokes	指	指	指	

次	丶	ン	丷	SHI, JI; *tsugi*, next; *tsu(gu)*, to rank next to
	沪	沪	次	次第 *shidai*, order, reason, as soon as
227 6 strokes				次官 *jikan*, vice-minister 目次 *mokuji*, table of contents

寺	一	十	土	JI; *tera* [*dera*], temple
	圭	寺	寺	寺院 *ji-in*, Buddhist temple 山寺 *yamadera*, mountain temple
228 6 strokes				

自	丿	亻	白	JI, SHI; *mizuka(ra)*, self, in person
	白	自	自	自分 *jibun*, self 自信 *jishin*, confidence
229 6 strokes				自由 *jiyū*, freedom

事	一	一	戸	JI; *koto*, thing, action, affair, fact
	戸	弖	弖	仕事 *shigoto*, work 用事 *yōji*, business 大事 *daiji*, great matter, serious affair, importance
230 8 strokes	弖	事		

持	一	十	扌	JI; *mo(chi)*, durability; *mo(tsu)*, to have, to hold
	扩	扩	拃	気持 *kimochi*, feeling 持参 *jisan*, bringing 支持 *shiji*, support
231 9 strokes	拃	持	持	

室	丶	宀	宀	SHITSU, room; *muro*, storeroom, cave
	宀	宏	宏	教室 *kyōshitsu*, classroom 室内 *shitsunai*, indoors 温室 *onshitsu*, hothouse, greenhouse
232 9 strokes	宓	室	室	

実	丶	宀	宀	JITSU, reality; *mi*, nut, fruit; *mino(ru)*, to bear fruit
	宀	宁	宝	実際 *jissai*, actual state, reality 真実 *shinjitsu*, truth 果実 *kajitsu*, fruit
233 8 strokes	宇	実		

社	丶	ラ	ネ	SHA [JA], a company; *yashiro*, Shintō shrine
	ネ	ネ	社	社会 *shakai*, society, the world, the community 会社 *kaisha*, (business) company 神社 *jinja*, shrine
234 7 strokes	社			

者	一	十	土	SHA; *mono*, person
	耂	耂	者	若者 *wakamono*, young man 医者 *isha*, doctor 学者 *gakusha*, scholar
235 **8 strokes**	者	者		

弱	フ	ㄱ	弓	JAKU; *yowa(i)*, weak; *yowa(ru)*, to grow weak, to be perplexed
	弓	引	弓⁷	弱虫 *yowamushi*, weakling 弱音 *yowane*, complaints 貧弱 *hinjaku*, scantiness, meager-
236 **10 strokes**	弜	弱	弱	ness

主	ヽ	二	宁	SHU, SU; *nushi*, master, owner
	亠	主		主人 *shujin*, master 民主主義 *minshushugi*, democracy 持主 *mochinushi*, owner
237 **5 strokes**				

取	一	「	F	SHU; *to(ru)*, to take
	F	耳	耳	取り出す *toridasu*, to take out 取材 *shuzai*, choice of subject 取扱い *toriatsukai*, treatment,
238 **8 strokes**	取	取		handling

首	ヽ	ソ	丷	SHU; *kubi*, neck
	丷	产	首	首輪 *kubiwa*, collar (dog) 手首 *tekubi*, wrist 首府 *shufu*, capital
239 **9 strokes**	首	首	首	

受	⺈	⺈	⺈	JU; u(ke), popularity, receptacle; u(keru), to receive
	⺈	⺈	⺈	受持 ukemochi, charge, matter in hand
				受付 uketsuke, receptionist, information desk
240 8 strokes	受	受		受話機 juwaki, telephone receiver

終	⺃	⺃	⺃	SHŪ; o(wari), end; o(waru), to come to an end; o(eru), to finish
	糸	糸	糸	終戦 shūsen, end of a war
				終業 shūgyō, end of work
241 11 strokes	終	終	終	最終 saishū, the last (糸 83)

週	)	刀	円	SHŪ, week
	円	円	周	週刊誌 shūkanshi, weekly magazine
				来週 raishū, next week
	⻌	週	週	今週 konshū, this week
242 11 strokes				(口 27)

集	)	イ	イ	SHŪ; atsu(meru), to collect (v.t.); atsu(maru), to gather together (v.i.)
	广	什	件	編集 henshū, editing
				詩集 shishū, anthology of poems
	隹	隹	集	文集 bunshū, literary anthology
243 12 strokes				(木 15)

住	)	イ	イ	JŪ, dwelling; su(mu), to dwell, to live
	亻	什	住	住所 jūsho, address
				衣食住 i-shoku-jū, necessities of life (clothing, food, shelter)
244 7 strokes	住			住宅 jūtaku, dwelling, living quarters

63

重 245 9 strokes	JŪ, CHŌ; *omo(i)*, heavy; *kasa-(neru)*, to pile (things) up; *kasa-(naru)*, to be piled up; ~*e*, ~fold 体重 *taijū*, weight (of the body) 厳重 *genjū*, strictness 二重 *futae*, *nijū*, duplicate, double, twofold
所 246 8 strokes	SHO (JO); *tokoro* [*dokoro*], place 台所 *daidokoro*, kitchen 場所 *basho*, place 近所 *kinjo*, neighborhood
暑 247 12 strokes	SHO; *atsu(i)*, hot 残暑 *zansho*, lingering summer heat 避暑 *hisho*, summering, going to a summer resort 暑中 *shochū*, midsummer (土 17)
助 248 7 strokes	JO; *tasu(karu)*, to be aided, to be rescued; *tasu(keru)*, to aid, to rescue; ~*suke*, suffix for masculine names 助手 *joshu*, assistant 補助 *hojo*, assistance 助力 *joryoku*, help, aid
昭 249 9 strokes	SHŌ (bright) 昭和 *Shōwa*, p.n., name of the present era in Japan

勝	月 月 月' 月' 月' 胖 朕 胖 勝	**SHŌ**; *ka(tsu)*, to win 勝負　*shōbu*, victory or defeat, match 勝敗　*shōhai*, the issue (of a battle) 勝手　*katte*, selfish, willful (月 12)
250 12 strokes		

乗	ノ 二 三 丢 岳 岳 垂 乖 乗	**JŌ**; *no(ru)*, to ride; *no(seru)*, to give a ride to, to place upon 乗り物　*norimono*, vehicle 乗客　*jōkyaku*, passenger 遠乗り　*tōnori*, a long ride
251 9 strokes		

場	一 十 土 圹 垣 垣 塴 場 場	**JŌ**; *ba*, place 工場　*kōjō, kōba*, factory 場所　*basho*, place 仕事場　*shigotoba*, place of work (土 11)
252 12 strokes		

食	ノ 人 介 今 今 今 食 食 食	**SHOKU**, food; *ta(beru)*, to eat; *ku(u)*, to eat 食物　*shokumotsu*, food, edibles 食堂　*shokudō*, dining hall 食事　*shokuji*, a meal 食
253 9 strokes		

申	丶 口 日 日 申	**SHIN**; *mō(su)*, to say 申し込み　*mōshikomi*, application, proposal 申告　*shinkoku*, report, filing a return 申し合わせ　*mōshiawase*, arrangement
254 5 strokes		

65

身 255 7 strokes	ノ イ 自 自 自 身 身	SHIN; *mi*, body 身体　*shintai*, body 身長　*shinchō*, height (of the body) 身分　*mibun*, social position
新 256 13 strokes	立 立 辛 辛 亲 亲 新 新 新	SHIN; *atara(shii)*, new; *ara(ta-ni)*, newly, afresh 新聞　*shimbun*, newspaper 新年　*shinnen*, the New Year 新学期　*shingakki*, new school term (立 149)
神 257 9 strokes	` ラ ネ ネ ネ 初 初 初 神	SHIN, JIN; *kami [gami]*, god 神経質　*shinkeishitsu*, nervous temperament 精神　*seishin*, soul, spirit 神様　*kamisama*, god
深 258 11 strokes	` ` 氵 氵 氵 氵 氵 深 深	SHIN; *fuka(i)*, deep, profound, thick (fog), close (connection); *fuka(sa)*, depth, profundity 深夜　*shin-ya*, midnight 深呼吸　*shinkokyū*, deep breath 深刻　*shinkoku*, serious, significant (木 15)
進 259 11 strokes	イ イ 亻 升 隹 隹 隹 進 進	SHIN; *susu(mu)*, to advance, to proceed 進行　*shinkō*, progress, advance 進級　*shinkyū*, promotion 行進　*kōshin*, march, parade (隹 集 243)

66

親	立 亲 亲	SHIN; *oya*, parent; *shita(shimu)*, to make friends with, to take kindly to; *shita(shii)*, intimate, familiar
	亲 新 亲	両親 *ryōshin*, parents
		親切 *shinsetsu*, kindness
260	親 親 親	親類 *shinrui*, relative, relation
16 strokes		(立 149, 木 15)

図	丨 冂 冈	ZU, drawing, plan; TO; *haka(ru)*, to devise
	冈 図 図	図画 *zuga*, drawing, a picture
		地図 *chizu*, map
261	図	図書館 *toshokan*, library
7 strokes		

数	丷 米 米	SŪ [ZŪ]; *kazu*, number; *kazo-(eru)*, to count
	娄 娄 娄	数字 *sūji*, figure, numeral
		数学 *sūgaku*, mathematics
262	数 数 数	人数 *ninzū*, the number of people
13 strokes		(米 135)

世	一 十 卄	SE, SEI; *yo*, world, age, reign
	卄 世	世界 *sekai*, the world
		世紀 *seiki*, century
263		世間 *seken*, the world, society, life
5 strokes		

星	丶 冂 日	SEI, JŌ; *hoshi* [*boshi*], star
	日 戸 旦	星座 *seiza*, constellation
		火星 *kasei*, Mars
264	旱 星 星	明星 *myōjō*, Venus
9 strokes		

晴
265
12 strokes

SEI; *ha(re)*, fine weather; *ha(reru)*, to clear (weather), to be dispelled

秋晴れ *akibare*, clear autumn weather
晴れ着 *haregi*, one's best clothes
晴天 *seiten*, fine weather

(月 12)

船
266
11 strokes

SEN; *fune* [*bune*], *funa*, boat, ship

渡し船 *watashi-bune*, ferry
船員 *sen-in*, sailor
汽船 *kisen*, steamboat, steamship

(口 27)

全
267
6 strokes

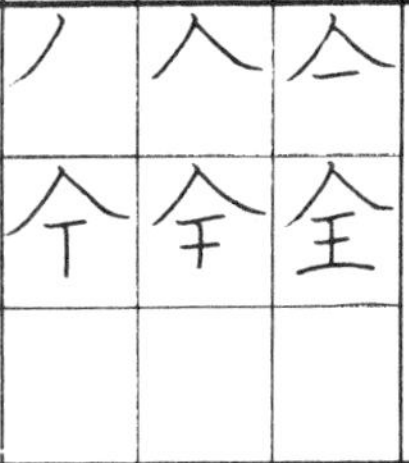

ZEN (whole); *matta(ku)*, entirely

全体 *zentai*, the whole
全部 *zembu*, all, the whole
完全 *kanzen*, perfect

送
268
9 strokes

SŌ; *oku(ru)*, to send

放送 *hōsō*, (radio) broadcast
輸送 *yusō*, transportation
送金 *sōkin*, sending money

太
269
4 strokes

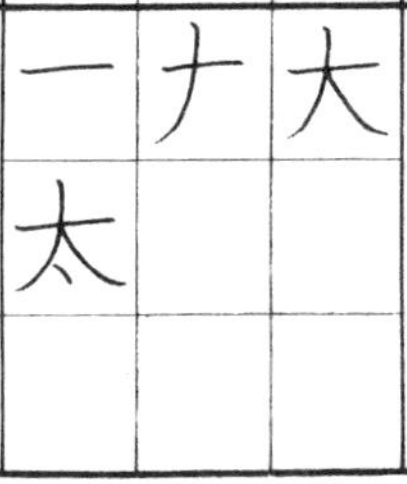

TAI, TA; *futo(i)*, big, deep (voice), bold (lines), shameless; *futo(ru)*, to grow fat

太陽 *taiyō*, sun
丸太 *maruta*, log
太平洋 *Taiheiyō*, Pacific Ocean

体 270 7 strokes	ノ イ 仁 什 仕 休 体	**TAI, TEI** (body) 体育 *tai-iku*, physical education 団体 *dantai*, a group 車体 *shatai*, body of a vehicle
待 271 9 strokes	´ ´ 彳 彳 彳 待 待 待 待	**TAI**; *ma(tsu)*, to wait for 待合室 *machiaishitsu*, waiting room 接待 *settai*, reception 招待 *shōtai*, invitation
台 272 5 strokes	ㄥ ム ム 台 台	**TAI; DAI**, a stand 台風 *taifū*, typhoon 舞台 *butai*, stage 燈台 *tōdai*, lighthouse
第 273 11 strokes	ノ ⺊ ⺋ ⺮ 竹 笂 笃 第 第	**DAI** (grade), prefix for ordinal numbers 第一回 *dai-ikkai*, the first time 及第 *kyūdai*, passing an examination 落第 *rakudai*, failure (in an examination), rejection
炭 274 9 strokes	⼁ 山 山 屵 屵 屵 炭 炭 炭	**TAN**; *sumi*, charcoal 炭坑 *tankō*, coal mine 石炭 *sekitan*, coal 木炭 *mokutan*, charcoal

69

		CHA, tea, tea plant
茶	一 十 艹 ア 芴 苯 芩 苶 茶	茶色　*cha-iro*, light brown 茶の湯　*cha-no-yu*, tea ceremony 茶わん　*chawan*, teacup, rice bowl
275 9 strokes		

		CHAKU; *ki(ru)*, to wear; *tsu(ku)*, to reach, to arrive
着	` ` `` ` ` ` ` ` ` ソ 羊 羊 羊 着 着	着物　*kimono*, Japanese robe 一着　*itchaku*, first arrival, a suit (of clothes) 上着　*uwagi*, coat (目 25)
276 12 strokes		

		CHŪ; *soso(gu)*, to pour, to concentrate on
注	` ` `` ` ` ` ` ` ジ 汁 汁 汼 注	注意　*chūi*, attention, care, warning, advice 注目　*chūmoku*, attention, observation 注文　*chūmon*, order, request, demand
277 8 strokes		

		CHŪ; *hashira [bashira]*, post, pillar
柱	一 十 オ 木 杧 杧 杧 柱 柱	帆柱　*hobashira*, mast 柱時計　*hashiradokei*, wall clock 電柱　*denchū*, telegraph (electric) pole
278 9 strokes		

		CHŪ; *hiru*, noon, daytime
昼	コ コ 尸 尺 尺 尽 昼 昼 昼	昼間　*hiruma*, daytime 昼夜　*chūya*, day and night 昼食　*chūshoku*, noon meal, lunch
279 9 strokes		

追 280 9 strokes	ノ イ 仆 戸 戸 自 `自 追 追	**TSUI**; *o(u)*, to run after, to drive away 追いかける　*oikakeru*, to chase 追求　　　*tsuikyū*, pursuit 追放　　　*tsuihō*, banishment, exile, purge
通 281 10 strokes	⁊ マ マ 乛 甬 甬 `甬 涌 通	**TSŪ**; *tō(ru)*, to go along, to pass; *kayo(u)*, to go to and from (a place) 大通り　　*ō-dōri*, main street 通信　　　*tsūshin*, correspondence, communication 通訳　　　*tsūyaku*, interpreter (用 146)
弟 282 7 strokes	` ゛ 当 当 弟 弟 弟	**TEI, DAI**; *otōto*, younger brother 兄弟　*kyōdai*, brothers 弟妹　*teimai*, younger brothers and sisters
鉄 283 13 strokes	入 合 金 金 釘 釕 釷 鉄 鉄	**TETSU**, iron, steel 鉄道　　　*tetsudō*, railroad 地下鉄　　*chikatetsu*, subway 鉄橋　　　*tekkyō*, iron bridge, railway bridge (金 16)
店 284 8 strokes	` 广 广 广 广 店 店	**TEN**; *mise*, store 店番　*miseban*, tending a store 商店　*shōten*, store (shop) 売店　*baiten*, stand, stall

71

点	⺊	⺊	⺊	**TEN**, point, marks, dot
	占	占	占	点数　*tensū*, merit marks 点字　*tenji*, braille points 決勝点　*kesshōten*, goal
285 9 strokes	点	点	点	

電	一	一	二	**DEN** (lightning, electricity)
	雨	雨	雨	電気　*denki*, electricity 電話　*denwa*, telephone 電報　*dempō*, telegram
286 13 strokes	雷	雷	電	(雨　42)

都	土	耂	耂	**TO, TSU**; *miyako*, capital, metropolis
	者	者	者	都会　*tokai*, city 首都　*shuto*, capital 都合　*tsugō*, circumstances, conditions
287 11 strokes	者	都	都	(土　17)

度	丶	亠	广	**DO**, degree, time, times
	广	庐	庐	一度　*ichido*, once 速度　*sokudo*, speed 程度　*teido*, degree, level, extent
288 9 strokes	庐	度	度	

刀	フ	刀		**TŌ**; *katana* [*gatana*], sword
				小刀　*kogatana*, pocketknife 大刀　*daitō*, long sword 軍刀　*guntō*, sabre
289 2 strokes				

当	⼁	⺌	⺌
	⺌	当	当
290 6 strokes			

TŌ; a(taru), to hit, to be equal to, to win (v.i.); a(teru), to hit, to apply, to guess (v.t.)

見当　kentō, guess
手当　teate, treatment, allowance
当然　tōzen, justly, naturally

投	一	十	扌
	扌	扒	投
	投		
291 7 strokes			

TŌ; na(geru), to throw, to give up

投票　tōhyō, voting
投資　tōshi, investment
投書　tōsho, contribution (to a magazine, newspaper, etc.)

島	⼁	冖	白
	白	帛	鳥
	鳥	島	島
292 10 strokes			

TŌ; shima [jima], island

半島　hantō, peninsula
群島　guntō, group of islands
島国　shimaguni, island country

(山 38)

答	ノ	⺊	⺊
	竹	竹	竺
	答	答	答
293 12 strokes			

TŌ [DŌ]; kota(e), answer; kota-(eru), to answer

答案　tōan, examination paper
問答　mondō, questions and answers
解答　kaitō, answer, solution

(竹 113, 口 27)

頭	一	豆	豆
	豆	豆	豆
	豆	頭	頭
294 16 strokes			

TŌ [DŌ], ZU; atama, head, top, brain

先頭　sentō, leader, head
教頭　kyōtō, head teacher
頭痛　zutsū, headache

(貝 169)

同	丨	冂	冂	DŌ; *ona(ji)*, same
	冋	同	同	同時 *dōji*, the same time
				同情 *dōjō*, sympathy
295				一同 *ichidō*, all (of us, them), all
6 strokes				the persons concerned

動	ニ	台	重	DŌ; *ugo(ku)*, to move
	重	重	動	動物 *dōbutsu*, animal
				自動車 *jidōsha*, automobile
296	動			運動 *undō*, motion, physical ex-
11 strokes				ercise, athletic sports
				(重 245)

肉	丨	冂	内	NIKU, meat, flesh
	内	肉	肉	牛肉 *gyūniku*, beef
				筋肉 *kinniku*, muscles
297				肉屋 *nikuya*, butcher, butcher
6 strokes				shop

波	`	⸜	氵	HA; *nami*, wave
	氵	沪	沪	大波 *ō-nami*, big wave
	波	波		防波堤 *bōhatei*, breakwater
298				電波 *dempa*, electric wave
8 strokes				

配	一	冂	丙	HAI [PAI]; *kuba(ru)*, to distribute,
	酉	酉	酉	to deliver
				配給 *haikyū*, ration, distribution
	酉フ	酉コ	配	(of food or goods)
299				配達 *haitatsu*, delivery
10 strokes				心配 *shimpai*, worry

買 300 12 strokes	丶 口 口	BAI; *ka(u)*, to buy, to purchase

買 300 12 strokes

	丶	冖	罒
	罒	四	罒
買い手	罒	買	

BAI; *ka(u)*, to buy, to purchase

売買 *baibai*, purchase and sale, buying and selling
買い物 *kaimono*, shopping
買い手 *kaite*, buyer
(貝 169)

| 売 301 7 strokes | 一 十 士 士 壳 声 声 売 | BAI; *u(ri)*, sale; *u(ru)*, to sell

売り出し *uridashi*, opening sale, bargain sale
商売 *shōbai*, business
発売 *hatsubai*, sale |

| 畑 302 9 strokes | 丶 丷 丷 火 灯 灯 烟 烟 畑 | *hata*, *hatake* [*batake*], field, farm, cultivated field

田畑 *tahata*, fields
麦畑 *mugibatake*, wheat (barley) field
花畑 *hanabatake*, flower garden |

| 発 303 9 strokes | フ ヌ ヌ 癶 癶 癶 癶 癶 発 | HATSU [PATSU] (to expose, to open, to shoot, to happen)

発音 *hatsuon*, pronunciation
発表 *happyō*, announcement
出発 *shuppatsu*, departure |

| 坂 304 7 strokes | 一 十 土 圢 圻 坂 坂 | HAN; *saka* [*zaka*], slope, hill

坂道 *sakamichi*, sloping road
上り坂 *noborizaka*, ascent, uphill road
急坂 *kyūhan*, steep slope |

75

板	一	十	才	HAN [BAN]; *ita*, board (of wood) 板の間 *ita-no-ma*, wooden floor 掲示板 *keijiban*, notice-board 看板 *kamban*, poster, signboard, shingle
305 8 strokes	木	杞	朽	
	析	板		

番	⸝	⸝	⸝⸝	BAN, number, guard, order, (one's) turn 番組 *bangumi*, program 交番 *kōban*, police-box 順番 *jumban*, order, one's turn (田 40)
306 12 strokes	立	平	釆	
	釆	番	番	

皮	)	厂	广	HI; *kawa* [*gawa*], skin, leather 毛皮 *kegawa*, fur 皮肉 *hiniku*, irony 皮膚 *hifu*, skin
307 5 strokes	皮	皮		

美	ヽ	⸝⸝	⸝⸝	BI, beauty; *utsuku(shii)*, beautiful 美術 *bijutsu*, fine arts 美人 *bijin*, a beauty, pretty girl, beautiful woman 美術館 *bijutsukan*, art museum
308 9 strokes	犬	羊	羊	
	美	美	美	

表	一	十	丰	HYŌ [PYŌ], list, table, schedule; *omote*, the outside, surface; *ara-(wasu)*, to show, to indicate, to expose, to express, to represent 表紙 *hyōshi*, cover of a book 表面 *hyōmen*, surface 時間表 *jikanhyō*, schedule, time-table
309 8 strokes	主	丰	表	
	表	表		

病 **310** 10 strokes	亠 广 疒 病	广 疒 病	广 疒 病	BYŌ; *yamai*, illness; *ya(mu)*, to fall ill 病気 *byōki*, illness, sickness 病院 *byōin*, hospital 病人 *byōnin*, sick person
品 **311** 9 strokes	丶 口 口 品	口 口 品	口 口 品	HIN, elegance, dignity; *shina*, goods 品物 *shinamono*, article, goods 手品 *tejina*, jugglery, sleight of hand 作品 *sakuhin*, work, works
負 **312** 9 strokes	ノ ク 負	ク 各 負	ク 各 負	FU [BU]; *o(u)*, to bear, to be indebted to; *ma(ke)*, a defeat; *ma(keru)*, to lose, to be defeated, to reduce in price, to make cheaper 勝負 *shōbu*, victory or defeat, game 負傷 *fushō*, wound 背負う *se-ou*, to carry on one's back
物 **313** 8 strokes	ノ 牛 物	㇄ 牛 物	牛 牜	BUTSU, MOTSU; *mono*, thing, article, object 食べ物 *tabemono*, food 名物 *meibutsu*, noted product, special product 貨物 *kamotsu*, freight
聞 **314** 14 strokes	丨 門 門	冂 門 門	冂 門 聞	BUN; *ki(ku)*, to hear, to listen to, to ask, to obey; *ki(koeru)*, to be heard 新聞 *shimbun*, newspaper 新聞社 *shimbunsha*, newspaper office 見聞 *kembun*, information, experience (耳 26)

77

平	一	一	一	HEI, BYŌ; *tai(ra)*, evenness, flatness; *hira(tai)*, even, level, simple
	平	平		平和 *heiwa*, peace
315 **5 strokes**				平気 *heiki*, calmness, indifference 平等 *byōdō*, equality
返	一	厂	万	HEN; *kae(su)*, to return, to give back; *kae(shi)* [*gae(shi)*]
	反	返	返	返事 *henji*, answer 繰り返す *kurikaesu*, to repeat
316 **7 strokes**	返			恩返し *ongaeshi*, repayment of a favor, returning a favor
勉	ノ	ク	ク	BEN (to exert oneself, to make efforts)
	各	各	各	勉強 *benkyō*, study 勤勉 *kimben*, diligence
317 **10 strokes**	免	免	勉	勉強家 *benkyōka*, studious person (力 148)
毎	ノ	厂	仁	MAI, every (prefix)
	勾	毎	毎	毎日 *mainichi*, every day 毎朝 *mai-asa*, every morning
318 **6 strokes**				毎週 *maishū*, every week
妹	く	夕	女	MAI; *imōto*, younger sister
	女	女	妖	弟妹 *teimai*, younger brothers and sisters
319 **8 strokes**	妹	妹		姉妹 *shimai*, sisters

万	一	フ	万	**MAN**, ten thousand; **BAN**
				万年筆 *mannenhitsu*, fountain pen
				万一 *man-ichi*, if by any chance
				万国 *bankoku*, all countries
320 3 strokes				

鳴	ロ	ロˊ	叮	**MEI**; *na(ku)*, to sing (birds), to cry (animals), to howl (animals), to chirp (insects)
	叭	呐	咱	鳴き声 *nakigoe*, cry (of animals)
				悲鳴 *himei*, scream, cry of distress
321 14 strokes	鳴	鳴	鳴	鳴動 *meidō*, rumbling
				(口 27, 灬 点 285)

面	一	丆	丆	**MEN**, side, phase, mask; *omote*, face, outside, front, surface; *omo* (lit.), face, surface
	丙	而	而	表面 *hyōmen*, surface
322 9 strokes	而	面	面	正面 *shōmen*, the front
				場面 *bamen*, scene

野	ﾉ	ﾛ	日	**YA**; *no*, field, plain
	甲	里	里	野原 *nohara*, field
				野球 *yakyū*, baseball
323 11 strokes	野	野	野	野外 *yagai*, outdoors

役	ノ	ﾌ	彳	**YAKU**, office, duty, role, use, service; **EKI** (lit.), war
	彳	役	役	役所 *yakusho*, public office
				役人 *yakunin*, government official
324 7 strokes	役			役者 *yakusha*, actor, actress

79

由	丶	冂	巾	YŪ, YU; *yoshi*, a reason, significance
	由	由		自由　*jiyū*, liberty, freedom
325 5 strokes				不自由　*fujiyū*, inconvenience, discomfort 理由　*riyū*, reason

遊	丶	亠	方	YŪ; *aso(bu)*, to play, to be idle
	方	方	方	遊星　*yūsei*, planet 遊戯　*yūgi*, game, sports, children's play
326 12 strokes	斿	斿	遊	遊覧　*yūran*, excursion, sightseeing (子 31, ⻌ 近 195)

葉	一	十	艹	YŌ; *ha* [*ba*], leaves, foliage
	艹	芏	苩	葉緑素　*yōryokuso*, chlorophyll 落ち葉　*ochiba*, fallen leaves
327 12 strokes	苃	葉	葉	葉巻　*hamaki*, cigar (木 15)

様	木	朾	栏	YŌ, way, style, manner; *sama*, Mr., Mrs., Miss, etc. (polite suffix for personal names); state, way, form, condition
	栏	栏	样	神様　*kamisama*, god 様子　*yōsu*, appearance, manner, state
328 14 strokes	样	様	様	(木 15)

曜	丨	冂	日	YŌ (term used for days of the week)
	日	日	日	木曜日　*mokuyōbi*, Thursday 土曜日　*doyōbi*, Saturday
329 18 strokes	日ヨ	日ヨヨ	曜	水曜日　*suiyōbi*, Wednesday (𦍌 243)

落 330 12 strokes	一 サ サ サ 芡 茨 落	十 サ 艺 茨	艹 艾 艺 落	RAKU; *o(chiru)*, to fall (v.i.), to be omitted, to be inferior to; *o(to-su)*, to let drop, to lose (v.t.), to omit, to make worse 落第 *rakudai*, failure (in an examination), rejection 落成 *rakusei*, completion (building, etc.) (口 27)
楽 331 13 strokes	′ 白 泊′	′ 白 泊	白 泊 楽	GAKU, music; RAKU, comfort, ease; *tano(shii)*, pleasant 楽しみ *tanoshimi*, pleasure 音楽会 *ongakukai*, concert, musicale 気楽 *kiraku*, ease, comfort (木 15)
里 332 7 strokes	丶 日 里	口 甲	日 里	RI, Japanese linear unit (2.44 miles); *sato* [*zato*], village, country, one's native home (usually as viewed by a woman married into another family) 郷里 *kyōri*, one's native place, home 村里 *murazato*, village 一里 *ichiri*, one ri
理 333 11 strokes	一 王 珇	丁 珂 理	干 珂 理	RI, reason, logic 理解 *rikai*, understanding 整理 *seiri*, arrangement, adjustment 料理 *ryōri*, cooking (里 332)
流 334 10 strokes	′ 汁 法	′ 法 流	氵 浐 流	RYŪ, RU; *naga(re)*, stream, current, flow; *naga(reru)*, to flow (v.i.); *naga(su)*, to set afloat, to wash away, to pour (v.t.) 流れ星 *nagareboshi*, shooting star 流行 *ryūkō*, fashion, vogue 電流 *denryū*, electric current

旅	亠	方	方	RYO; *tabi*, travel, journey
	方	扩	扩	旅人　*tabibito*, traveler 旅行　*ryokō*, trip, travel 旅館　*ryokan*, inn, hotel
335 10 strokes	扩	扩	旅	(方　138)

両	一	一	冂	RYŌ, old Japanese monetary unit, (two, both)
	両	両	両	両手　*ryōte*, both hands 両方　*ryōhō*, both, both sides 両親　*ryōshin*, parents, father and mother
336 6 strokes				

礼	`	ラ	ネ	REI, salutation, courtesy, bow, thanks
	ネ	礼		礼儀　*reigi*, courtesy, manners, etiquette 無礼　*burei*, impoliteness, discourtesy ⌈ness 失礼　*shitsurei*, discourtesy, rude-
337 5 strokes				

和	ノ	二	千	WA, harmony, peace, (Japan); *ya-wa(ragu)*, to soften, to calm down (v.i.)
	禾	禾	和	平和　*heiwa*, peace 和服　*wafuku*, Japanese clothes, kimono 調和　*chōwa*, harmony
338 8 strokes	和	和		

愛	ノ	⺈	⺗	AI, love; *ai(suru)*, to love
	爫	尚	恶	愛情　*aijō*, love, affection 愛国心　*aikokushin*, patriotism 愛児　*aiji*, one's beloved child
339 13 strokes	愛	愛	愛	(心　95,　⺈　受　240)

82

案

340
10 strokes

AN, plan, idea; *an(jiru)*, to be anxious about, to be concerned about

案外 *angai*, unexpectedly
案内 *annai*, guide, guidance
名案 *meian*, good idea, good plan

(木 15)

衣

341
6 strokes

I; *koromo*, clothes, garment, priest's robe

衣類 *irui*, clothing
衣食住 *i-shoku-jū*, clothing, food and shelter
衣替え *koromogae*, change of dress

以

342
5 strokes

I (with, through, on account of)

以上 *ijō*, above, more than
以外 *igai*, besides, outside of
以前 *izen*, before, formerly

囲

343
7 strokes

I; *kako(mu)*, to surround

胸囲 *kyōi*, girth of the chest, chest measurement
周囲 *shūi*, circumference, surroundings
範囲 *han-i*, extent, sphere, limits

位

344
7 strokes

I; *kurai*, rank, position, grade; about (approximately)

地位 *chi-i*, rank, social standing
位置 *ichi*, location, situation
学位 *gaku-i*, academic degree

医 345 7 strokes	一 ⼂ 三 匸 チ 天	戸 天 丐 医	I (to heal, to cure) 医者 *isha*, physician, doctor 医学 *igaku*, medical science 医院 *i-in*, medical practitioner's office
委 346 8 strokes	千 二 千 禾 千 委	禾 禾	I (to entrust with) 委員 *i-in*, committee, delegate 委員長 *i-inchō*, chairman of a committee 委任 *i-nin*, charge, trust, commission
育 347 8 strokes	、 亠 云 云 亠 育 亡 亠 育	育 育	IKU; *soda(teru)*, to bring up, to educate, to raise 教育 *kyōiku*, education 体育 *tai-iku*, physical education 育児 *ikuji*, upbringing of a child
印 348 6 strokes	ノ イ 仁 仁 臼 印		IN, seal, stamp; *shirushi* [*jirushi*], sign, symbol, trace 印刷 *insatsu*, printing 矢印 *yajirushi*, arrow sign 目印 *mejirushi*, mark
員 349 10 strokes	、 冂 口 尸 月 員 員 員	員	IN (member, official, personnel) 満員 *man-in*, no vacancy, full house 一員 *ichi-in*, (one) member 職員 *shokuin*, staff, personnel

院 350 10 strokes	フ	３	阝
	阝ʼ	阝ʼ	阝宀
	阢	阰	院

IN (temple, academy, board), suffix for "institution"

病院　　*byōin*, hospital
美容院　*biyōin*, beauty shop
下院　　*ka-in*, House of Representatives, Lower House

(元 68)

飲 351 12 strokes	𠆢	今	仝
	食	食	飠
	飮	飲	飲

IN; *no(mu)* to drink

飲料水　*inryōsui* drinking water
飲み水　*nomimizu*, drinking water
飲み物　*nomimono*, drinks

(食 253)

泳 352 8 strokes	丶	冫	氵
	氵	汀	汀
	泳	泳	

EI; *oyo(gu)*, to swim

水泳　　　　*suiei*, swimming
平泳ぎ　　　*hira-oyogi*, breast stroke
水泳大会　　*suiei taikai*, swimming meet

英 353 8 strokes	一	十	艹
	艹	艻	苂
	苵	英	

EI (England, excellent)

英語　*eigo*, English language
英雄　*eiyū*, hero
日英　*Nichi-Ei*, Japan and England

塩 354 13 strokes	土	圵	圹
	垆	垳	塩
	塩	塩	塩

EN; *shio*, salt

塩水　*shiomizu*, salt water
塩田　*enden*, salt bed
食塩　*shokuen*, table salt

(土 17, 口 27)

85

横	木	朴	林	**Ō**; *yoko*, the side, the width
	杧	構	横	横書き *yokogaki*, writing from left to right
355 15 strokes	横	横	横	横断 *ōdan*, crossing, intersection 横顔 *yokogao*, side view of a person's face, profile (木 15, 由 325)

加	フ	力	加	**KA**; *kuwa(eru)*, to add, to join, to increase (v.t.); *kuwa(waru)*, to join, to enter (v.i.)
	加	加		参加 *sanka*, participation
356 5 strokes				加入 *kanyū*, entrance, joining 増加 *zōka*, increase

貨	ノ	イ	イ′	**KA** (treasure, goods)
	化	仵	貨	百貨店 *hyakkaten*, department store
357 11 strokes	貨	貨	貨	銀貨 *ginka*, silver coin 雑貨 *zakka*, miscellaneous goods, sundries (貝 169)

芽	一	十	サ	**GA**; *me*, bud, sprout, shoot
	艹	芏	芽	木の芽 *ki-no-me*, leaf bud
358 7 strokes	芽	芽		新芽 *shimme*, sprout, bud, shoot 芽ばえ *mebae*, bud, sprout

改	フ	コ	己	**KAI**; *arata(meru)*, to change, to reform, to revise; *arata(maru)*, to be reformed
	己	改	改	改良 *kairyō*, improvement
359 7 strokes	改			改心 *kaishin*, conversion, reform 改札口 *kaisatsuguchi*, ticket gate

械	十	木	朾
360 11 strokes	朾	析	枅
	械	械	械

KAI (shackles)

機械 *kikai*, machine
器械 *kikai*, instrument, apparatus

階	フ	ヲ	阝
361 12 strokes	阝゙	阝ヒ	阝ピ
	阝比	階	階

KAI [GAI], story of a building, floor, grade

階段 *kaidan*, stairs, stairway
階級 *kaikyū*, class, caste
三階 *sangai*, 3rd floor

(白 37)

害	丶	丷	宀
362 10 strokes	宀	宇	宇
	宝	害	

GAI, harm, calamity

害虫 *gaichū*, harmful insect
損害 *songai*, loss, damage
障害 *shōgai*, obstacle, hindrance

(口 27)

覚	丶	丷	丷
363 12 strokes	丷	宀	学
	覚	覚	覚

KAKU; *obo(eru)*, to remember, to understand

覚え書 *oboegaki*, memorandum, note「feeling
感覚 *kankaku*, sensation, sense,
自覚 *jikaku*, consciousness, self-consciousness

(目 25)

官	丶	丷	宀
364 8 strokes	宁	宁	官
	官	官	

KAN, government, government position

官庁 *kanchō*, government office
裁判官 *saibankan*, judge
警官 *keikan*, policeman, police officer

関	丨 門 門 閂	門 門 閂 関	門 門 関 関	**KAN**; *seki*, barrier 関心 *kanshin*, concern, interest 玄関 *genkan*, entrance hall, entrance 機関車 *kikansha*, engine, locomotive
365 14 strokes				(門 143)
館	𠆢 食 食	含 飣 館	食 飣 館	**KAN** (building, hall) 図書館 *toshokan*, library 映画館 *eigakan*, movie theater 旅館 *ryokan*, inn, hotel
366 16 strokes	館	館	館	(食 253, 官 364)
観	丿 午 午	仁 午 隹	午 午 観	**KAN** (to look at carefully, to show) 観光 *kankō*, sightseeing 観察 *kansatsu*, observation 観測 *kansoku*, observation, survey
367 18 strokes	奔	隹	観	(見 67)
願	一 厂 厂	厂 原 原	厂 原 原	**GAN**; *nega(i)*, wish, petition, request; *nega(u)*, to ask, to request, to wish, to beg 願書 *gansho*, written application 志願 *shigan*, volunteering, desire, application
368 19 strokes	原	原	願	(原 205, 貝 169)
季	一 二 千	千 禾 季		**KI**, season 季節 *kisetsu*, season 四季 *shiki*, the four seasons 雨季 *uki*, rainy season
369 8 strokes	季	季		

喜	一	十	士	KI; *yoroko(bi)*, joy, happy event, congratulation; *yoroko(bu)*, to rejoice, to be glad
	吉	吉	吉	大喜び　*ō-yorokobi*, great joy, great delight
370	壴	喜		喜劇　*kigeki*, comedy 歓喜　*kanki*, joy, ecstasy
12 strokes				(口 27)

旗	方	扩	扩	KI; *hata*, flag
	斻	旃	旃	国旗　*kokki*, national flag 校旗　*kōki*, school flag
371	旌	旗	旗	星条旗　*seijōki*, the Stars and Stripes
14 strokes				(方 138)

器	口	口口	吅	KI; *utsuwa*, vessel, utensil, capacity, caliber
	罘	哭	器	食器　*shokki*, tableware 陶器　*tōki*, pottery, ceramics
372	器			洗面器　*semmenki*, wash basin
15 strokes				(口 27)

機	木	杉	桦	KI; *hata*, loom
	样	样	楼	機械　*kikai*, machine, mechanism 機会　*kikai*, opportunity, chance
373	機	機	機	危機　*kiki*, crisis, emergency
16 strokes				(木 15, 幺 糸 83)

宮	丶	丷	宀	KYŪ, GŪ, KU; *miya*, shrine, prince (of the blood)
	宫	宀	宮	宮殿　*kyūden*, palace 神宮　*jingū*, Shintō shrine
374				宮様　*miya-sama*, royal prince
10 strokes				(口 27)

挙	`	``	```	KYO (to conduct, to perform)
	屶	产	兴	選挙 *senkyo*, election 挙行 *kyokō*, performance 挙手 *kyoshu*, raising one's hand, a show of hands
375 10 strokes	兴	巻	挙	(手 28)

共	一	十	廿	KYŌ; *tomo*, both, as well as, together
	业	共	共	共通 *kyōtsū*, commonness 共和国 *kyōwakoku*, republic
376 6 strokes				共産党 *kyōsantō*, Communist Party

協	一	十	十フ	KYŌ (to be in harmony)
	十カ	协	协	協力 *kyōryoku*, cooperation 協会 *kyōkai*, society, association
377 8 strokes	協	協		協議 *kyōgi*, conference, consultation

鏡	金	釕	鈩	KYŌ; *kagami*, mirror
	鍗	錞	錆	鏡台 *kyōdai*, dressing table, mirror stand 双眼鏡 *sōgankyō*, binoculars
378 19 strokes	鎧	鏡		顕微鏡 *kembikyō*, microscope (金 16, 立 149)

競	立	音	产	KYŌ, KEI; *kiso(u)*, to rival, to compete
	竞	竞立	竞音	競争 *kyōsō*, competition 競技 *kyōgi*, match, tournament, sporting events
379 20 strokes	競	競		競馬 *keiba*, horse race (立 149, ル 27) ·

業 380 13 strokes	丶 业 丵	丨 业 丵	川 业 業	GYŌ, occupation, business, industry, studies; GŌ, karma 職業 *shokugyō*, occupation, profession 産業 *sangyō*, industry 工業 *kōgyō*, industry, manufacturing industry
曲 381 6 strokes	丶 曱	冂 曲	巾 曲	KYOKU, melody; *ma(garu)*, to bend, to twist, to turn (v.i.); *ma-(geru)*, to bend, to twist, to turn (v.t.) 曲線 *kyokusen*, curved line 作曲 *sakkyoku*, musical composition 曲がり道 *magarimichi*, crooked road, winding lane
極 382 12 strokes	木 柯 極	杧 極	朽 極	KYOKU, terrestrial poles, magnetic poles, zenith; GOKU (very, extremely) 極端 *kyokutan*, extremity 北極 *hokkyoku*, North Pole 至極 *shigoku*, very, quite (木 15, 口 27)
具 383 8 strokes	丨 目 具	冂 且 具	月 且	GU, tool, utensil; ingredients 道具 *dōgu*, tool, utensil, instrument 具合 *guai*, condition, state 具体的 *gutaiteki*, concrete, definite
郡 384 10 strokes	﹁ 尹 君了	ヲ 君 郡	ヨ 君阝	GUN, county, district; *kōri* (lit.), county, district 郡部 *gumbu*, rural district, counties 郡長 *gunchō*, head of a county (口 27)

係	ノ	イ	イ	KEI; *kakari* [*gakari*], charge, duty, in charge (of); *kaka(ru)*, to affect, to concern
	仁	侉	侉	係員 *kakari-in*, clerk in charge 関係 *kankei*, relation, connection, participation, implication
385 9 strokes	俘	係	係	記録係 *kirokugakari*, person in charge of records, recorder

景	丶	口	日	KEI, KE (view, scene)
	日	早	豆	風景 *fūkei*, scenery, view 不景気 *fukeiki*, bad times, depression
386 12 strokes	昙	景	景	光景 *kōkei*, spectacle, scene (日 27)

軽	一	戸	亘	KEI; *karu* [*garu*], *karu(i)*, light (in weight), slight, easy
	車	軒	軻	軽卒 *keisotsu*, rashness, hastiness 軽音楽 *kei-ongaku*, light music
387 12 strokes	軺	軽	軽	気軽 *kigaru*, light-hearted (車 88)

芸	一	十	艹	GEI, arts, accomplishments
	艹	兰	芸	芸術 *geijutsu*, art 民芸 *mingei*, folk art 芸者 *geisha*, Japanese singing and dancing girl
388 7 strokes	芸			

血	ノ	イ	冖	KETSU; *chi*, blood
	向	血	血	血液 *ketsueki*, blood 出血 *shukketsu*, bleeding, hemorrhage
389 6 strokes				血管 *kekkan*, blood vessel

結	く	幺	幺	KETSU; *musu(bi)*, end, knot; *musu(bu)*, to tie, to bind, to conclude, to link; *yu(u)*, to dress (the hair)
	乡	糸	紀	結果 *kekka*, result 結婚 *kekkon*, marriage 連結 *renketsu*, coupling, connection, linking
390 12 strokes	紀	紵	結	(糸 83, 口 27)

建	⏋	⏋	⏋	KEN; *ta(teru)*, to build, to establish; *ta(tsu)*, to be built; ~*date*, ~-storied building
	⏋	聿	聿	建物 *tatemono*, a building 建築 *kenchiku*, construction, architecture, building
391 9 strokes	津	建		二階建 *nikaidate*, two-storied building

言	`	ニ	亠	GEN, GON, speech, statement; *koto*, word, speech, expression; *i(u)*, to say
	言	言	言	方言 *hōgen*, dialect
392 7 strokes	言			無言 *mugon*, silence, muteness 言葉 *kotoba*, word, language

固	⎮	冂	冂	KO; *kata(meru)*, to harden, to make hard (v.t.); *kata(maru)*, to become hard; *kata(i)*, hard, firm
	冊	甪	甪	固有 *koyū*, peculiar, one's own 固体 *kotai*, a solid (body)
393 8 strokes	固	固		強固 *kyōko*, firmness, solidity, stability

湖	`	⁝	氵	KO; *mizu-umi*, lake
	氵	汁	沽	湖水 *kosui*, lake 湖岸 *kogan*, shore of a lake 湖畔 *kohan*, border of a lake
394 12 strokes	泐	湖	湖	(口 27, 月 12)

93

幸

395
8 strokes

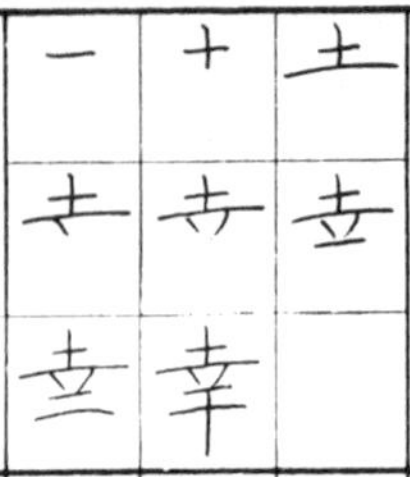

KŌ; *saiwa(i)*, blessings, good luck, happiness, fortune

不幸 *fukō*, unhappiness, misfortune
幸福 *kōfuku*, happiness
幸運 *kōun*, good fortune

航

396
10 strokes

KŌ (to sail on the water)

航海 *kōkai*, voyage, navigation
航路 *kōro*, sea route, air route
航空 *kōkū*, aviation, air voyage

港

397
12 strokes

KŌ; *minato*, harbor

港町 *minatomachi*, port town
入港 *nyūkō*, entry into port
空港 *kūkō*, airport

(氵 汽 60)

告

398
7 strokes

KOKU; *tsu(geru)*, to tell, to inform

報告 *hōkoku*, report
広告 *kōkoku*, advertisement
忠告 *chūkoku*, advice

差

399
10 strokes

SA, difference, remainder (math.); *sa(su)*, to thrust, to insert

差別 *sabetsu*, distinction, discrimination
大差 *taisa*, great difference
差出人 *sashidashinin*, sender, addresser

祭	`	ク	タ	SAI; *matsu(ri)*, festival; *matsu(ru)*, to deify, to worship as a god, to offer prayers for the sake of
	夕	列	叔	村祭り　*muramatsuri*, village festival 祭日　*saijitsu*, national holiday
400 11 strokes	欢	祭	祭	文化祭　*bunkasai*, cultural festival (示 622)

菜	一	十	艹	SAI; *na*, greens, rape (vegetable)
	艹	艾	艾	野菜　*yasai*, vegetables 菜の花　*na-no-hana*, rape blossoms 菜園　*saien*, vegetable garden
401 11 strokes	苎	茎	菜	(木 15)

最	日	旦	旱	SAI, prefix for forming superlatives; *motto(mo)*, most
	早	昌	昌	最初　*saisho*, the first, beginning 最後　*saigo*, the last
402 12 strokes	最	最	最	最善　*saizen*, the best (日 旱 104)

材	一	十	才	ZAI, material (for work), timber, ability, talent
	木	村	村	木材　*mokuzai*, lumber, wood 材料　*zairyō*, raw material, ingredients
403 7 strokes	材			人材　*jinzai*, capable man

昨	l	冂	日	SAKU (yesterday, ancient times)
	日	日'	旷	昨日　*sakujitsu*, yesterday 昨年　*sakunen*, last year
404 9 strokes	昨	昨	昨	昨夜　*sakuya*, last night

刷	コ	コ	尸	SATSU; su(ru), to print; ~zuri, suffix for " printing "
	尸	吊	吊	印刷　　　insatsu, printing 校正刷り　kōseizuri, proofs 　　　　　　(printing)
405 8 strokes	刷	刷		謄写版刷り　tōshaban-zuri, mimeographed copy

察	、	丷	宀	SATSU; sas(suru), to guess, to perceive, to sympathize with
	夕	如	如	観察　kansatsu, observation 視察　shisatsu, inspection 警察　keisatsu, police
406 14 strokes	疚	察	察	(祭 400)

散	一	十	廿	SAN; chi(ru), to fall (leaves), to be scattered (v.i.); chi(rasu), to scatter, to disperse (v.t.); ~san, suffix for " powder " (medicine)
	廿	苦	背	散歩　sampo, walk, stroll 解散　kaisan, breakup, dissolution
407 12 strokes	散	散	散	胃散　isan, medical powder for the stomach

産	丶	亠	立	SAN, childbearing, product, fortune; u(mu), to give birth to, to produce
	立	立	产	産物　sambutsu, products 産地　sanchi, place of production
408 11 strokes	产	产	産	産業　sangyō, industry (生 34)

残	一	ブ	万	ZAN; noko(ri), remainder; noko(ru), to be left over, to remain; noko(su), to leave, to save
	歹	歹	歹三	残念　zannen, regret, disappointment 残金　zankin, balance, money left over 「overs
409 10 strokes	残	残	残	残り物　nokorimono, remains, left-

| 士 | 一 十 士 | **SHI** (man, figure) |
| **410** 3 strokes | | 武士 *bushi*, samurai
紳士 *shinshi*, gentleman
勇士 *yūshi*, brave man, hero |

| 史 | 丶 ⼍ 口
史 史 | **SHI** (annals, history, chronicles) |
| **411** 5 strokes | | 歴史 *rekishi*, history
女史 *joshi*, Madame, Mrs., Miss
史上 *shijō*, in history, in the annals |

| 司 | ⼆ ⼆ 司
司 司 | **SHI** (to rule, to manage) |
| **412** 5 strokes | | 司会者 *shikaisha*, master of ceremonies, moderator, chairman
司令 *shirei*, order, command
司令部 *shireibu*, headquarters |

| 姉 | ⼃ ⼥ 女
女 女 女
姉 姉 | **SHI**; *ane*, elder sister |
| **413** 8 strokes | | 姉妹 *shimai, ane-imōto*, sisters
姉娘 *anemusume*, elder daughter
姉婿 *anemuko*, elder sister's husband |

| 歯 | ⼃ ⼘ 止
止 止 芈
米 歯 歯 | **SHI**; *ha [ba]*, tooth |
| **414** 12 strokes | | 虫歯 *mushiba*, decayed tooth
歯医者 *ha-isha*, dentist
歯車 *haguruma*, gear, cogwheel

(米 135) |

97

詩	`	`	`
	`言`	`言`	`計`
415 13 strokes	`計`	`詩`	`詩`

SHI, poetry, poem

詩人　　*shijin*, poet
詩集　　*shishū*, anthology of poetry
叙事詩　*jojishi*, epic poem

(口　27,　土　17)

試	`言`	`言`	`訂`
	`訂`	`試`	`試`
416 13 strokes	`試`		

SHI; *kokoro(mi)*, trial, test; *kokoro(miru)*, to try

試験　　*shiken*, examination
試運転　*shi-unten*, test driving, trial run
試合　　*shiai*, match, contest

(言　392)

式	`一`	`二`	`干`
	`工`	`式`	`式`
417 6 strokes			

SHIKI, ceremony, form, model; ~*shiki*, ~-style (suffix for "style," "type")

式場　　*shikijō*, ceremonial hall
卒業式　*sotsugyō-shiki*, graduation ceremony, commencement
旧式　　*kyūshiki*, old-style

失	`ノ`	` レ`	`ヒ`
	`失`	`失`	
418 5 strokes			

SHITSU; *ushina(u)*, to lose, to miss

失礼　*shitsurei*, impoliteness
失敗　*shippai*, failure
失望　*shitsubō*, despair, disappointment

写	`ノ`	`冖`	`冖`
	`写`	`写`	
419 5 strokes			

SHA; *utsu(su)*, to copy, to imitate, to take (a photograph)

写真　*shashin*, photograph
写生　*shasei*, sketch, drawing from nature
映写　*eisha*, projection

借 420 10 strokes	ノ イ 仁 什 仁 供 借 借 借	SHAKU; *ka(ri)*, borrowing, debt; *ka(riru)*, to borrow, to rent, to substitute temporarily, to obtain (help) 借金 *shakkin*, debt, loan 借り物 *karimono*, borrowed thing 拝借 *haishaku*, loan, borrowing (扌 11)
守 421 6 strokes	' ', 宀 宀 守 守	SHU, SU; *mamo(ru)*, to protect, to guard, to defend, to obey (the law), to keep (a promise) お守り *o-mamori*, amulet, charm 留守 *rusu*, absence 保守 *hoshu*, conservatism
酒 422 10 strokes	氵 氵 氵 氵 沔 酒 酒 酒	SHU; *sake* (*saka*), rice wine, liquor ぶどう酒 *budōshu*, wine 酒飲み *sakenomi*, drinker 酒屋 *sakaya*, liquor shop (氵 酉 60)
種 423 14 strokes	' ᷃ 千 禾 禾 种 秳 種 種	SHU (kind, sort); *tane*, seed 種まき *tanemaki*, sowing seed 種類 *shurui*, sort, kind 人種 *jinshu*, human race (重 245)
州 424 6 strokes	')) 丬 州 州	SHŪ, province, state (U.S.A.) 本州 *Honshū* (main island of Japan) 九州 *Kyūshū* (Japan's third largest island) ユタ州 *Yuta-shū*, State of Utah

99

拾 425 9 strokes	一 扌 扒 拾	十 扌 扒 拾	扌 扒 拾 拾	SHŪ; JŪ, ten (used in legal documents); *hiro(u)*, to pick up 拾い物 *hiroimono*, something picked up, windfall, bargain 命拾い *inochibiroi*, narrow escape (from death) 拾弐円 *jūni-en*, 12 yen
習 426 11 strokes	フ 羽羽 羽羽	ヲ 羽羽 羽羽	习 羽羽 習	SHŪ; *nara(u)*, to learn, to study 練習 *renshū*, practice 習字 *shūji*, penmanship 習慣 *shūkan*, habit, custom
順 427 12 strokes	丿 川 順	川 川 順	川 順 順	JUN, order, turn 順序 *junjo*, order, procedure, method 順番 *jumban*, order, turn 順調 *junchō*, normal condition, smooth progress (目 25)
初 428 7 strokes	丶 衤 初	ラ 衤	礻 初	SHO; *hatsu*, first; *haji(me)*, beginning 初秋 *shoshū*, early autumn 初雪 *hatsuyuki*, first snow of the year 初期 *shoki*, first stage
消 429 10 strokes	氵 沙 消	氵 沪 消	氵 消	SHŌ; *ki(eru)*, to vanish, to go out, to melt away; *ke(su)*, to extinguish, to switch off, to put out (a light) 消しゴム *keshigomu*, eraser 消防 *shōbō*, fire fighting 消毒 *shōdoku*, disinfection (氵 肖 60)

| 唱 430 11 strokes | 丶 口丿 口日 | 口 叮 叩 | 口 叮 唱 | SHŌ; *tona(eru)*, to chant, to recite, to say 独唱 *dokushō*, vocal solo 合唱 *gasshō*, chorus 唱歌 *shōka*, song, singing |

| 商 431 11 strokes | 丶 产 商 | 亠 产 商 | 亠 产 商 | SHŌ; *akina(u)*, to sell, to deal in 商人 *shōnin*, merchant 商売 *shōbai*, business, trade, transaction 商業 *shōgyō*, commerce, trade (口 27) |

| 章 432 11 strokes | 亠 音 音 | 立 音 章 | 立 音 | SHŌ, chapter 文章 *bunshō*, sentence 記章 *kishō*, medal, badge 勲章 *kunshō*, decoration, order (for honors) (立 149) |

| 照 433 13 strokes | 丨 日 昭 | 冂 日ヲ 昭 | 日 日刀 照 | SHŌ; *te(rasu)*, to shine on, to compare with, to shed light on; *te(ru)*, to shine 日照り *hideri*, drought 照明 *shōmei*, illumination 対照 *taishō*, contrast |

| 焼 434 12 strokes | 火 灶 焼 | 火ゝ 焼 焼 | 火十 焼 焼 | SHŌ; *ya(ku)*, to burn, to bake, to grill, to toast (v.t.), to burn with jealousy; *ya(keru)*, to be burned, to be roasted, to be jealous of 夕焼け *yūyake*, evening glow, sunset colors 焼失 *shōshitsu*, destruction by fire (火 13) |

101

植 435 12 strokes	一 十 才 木 杧 杧 枯 植 植	SHOKU; u(eru), to plant, to set up (type) 植物 shokubutsu, plant, vegetation 植民地 shokuminchi, colony 田植え taue, rice planting (H 25)
臣 436 7 strokes	㇐ 匚 匚 臣 臣 臣 臣	SHIN, JIN (retainer, subject) 大臣 daijin, cabinet minister 忠臣 chūshin, loyal retainer
信 437 9 strokes	ノ 亻 亻 亻 亻 信 信 信 信	SHIN, sincerity, trust, faith; shin(zuru), to believe, to trust, to believe in 信用 shin-yō, trust, confidence, belief, credit 信号 shingō, signal 通信 tsūshin, communication
真 438 10 strokes	一 十 亠 古 方 直 直 真 真	SHIN; ma, truth, reality 写真機 shashinki, camera 真夏 manatsu, midsummer
成 439 6 strokes	ノ 厂 万 成 成 成	SEI, JŌ; na(ru), to become, to be completed, to consist of, to come to, to succeed; to come, to go (honorific); na(su), to do, to perform 成長 seichō, growth 完成 kansei, completion 賛成 sansei, agreement, approval

清	シ	シー	汁	SEI ; *kiyo(i)*, *kiyo(raka)*, pure, clear
	汻	清	清	清潔　*seiketsu*, cleanliness 清書　*seisho*, fair copy 血清　*kessei*, (blood) serum
440 11 strokes	清	清	清	(氵 汽 60)

勢	土	幸	坴	SEI [ZEI] ; *ikio(i)*, force, vigor, power, influence
	坴	坴丿	執	勢力　*seiryoku*, power, influence 大勢　*taisei*, general trend ; *ōzei*, large number of people
441 13 strokes	執丸	勢	勢	軍勢　*gunzei*, number of soldiers, troops (土 17)

静	十	主	青	SEI, JŌ ; *shizu(ka)*, quiet, silent, peaceful ; *shizu(maru)*, to become quiet ; *shizu(meru)*, to make calm, to soothe
	青丿	青ク	青タ	静止　*seishi*, stillness, standstill 静物　*seibutsu*, still life
442 14 strokes	静	静	静	安静　*ansei*, complete rest (青 36)

整	一	戸	束	SEI ; *totono(eru)*, to put in order, to get ready ; *totono(u)*, to be ready
	束	束	束	整理　*seiri*, adjustment, arrangement, reorganization
443 16 strokes	束攵	敕	整	整備　*seibi*, adjustment, complete equipment, consolidation (口 27, 正 46)

席	丶	亠	广	SEKI, seat, place
	广	庐	庐	出席　*shusseki*, attendance, presence 欠席　*kesseki*, absence
444 10 strokes	庐	席	席	座席　*zaseki*, seat

103

積	禾	禾	利	SEKI, product (math.); *tsumo(ri)*, intention; *tsu(mu)*, to pile up, to load, to accumulate (v.t.); *tsumo-(ru)*, to be piled up
	秚	秚	秲	面積　　*menseki*, area 積極的　*sekkyokuteki*, positive, active, progressive
445 16 strokes	積	積		積荷　　*tsumini*, cargo, a load (貝 169, 禾 秋 89)
節	ノ	ト	ケ	SETSU, paragraph, season, time; *fushi*, joint, knot, tune
	ケケ	竹ケ	竺ケ	節約　*setsuyaku*, economy, frugality
446 13 strokes	館	節	節	調節　*chōsetsu*, regulation, control 使節　*shisetsu*, delegate, envoy
線	く	幺	糸	SEN, line, track, wire, string
	紀	絈	紳	地平線　*chiheisen*, horizon (on land) 光線　　*kōsen*, light, beam, ray
447 15 strokes	線	線	線	直線　　*chokusen*, straight line (糸 83, 白 37)
戦	ヽ	当	当	SEN; *tataka(i)*, fight, war, struggle; *tataka(u)*, to fight, to make war, to struggle, to compete in games
	単	単	戦	戦争　*sensō*, war 終戦　*shūsen*, end of a war
448 13 strokes	戦	戦		戦場　*senjō*, battlefield (単 671)
選	フ	コ	己	SEN; *era(bu)*, to choose, to select
	己	己	巽	選挙　*senkyo*, election 選手　*senshu*, player, champion
449 15 strokes	巽	選	選	当選　*tōsen*, victory in an election (共 376)

然	ノ	ク	タ	**ZEN, NEN** (yes, but, however)
	タ	外	狀	自然 *shizen*, nature 当然 *tōzen*, natural, just, as a matter of course
450 **12 strokes**	狀	狀	然	天然 *tennen*, nature (大 66)

争	ノ	ク	夕	**SŌ**; *araso(i)*, quarrel, dispute, competition; *araso(u)*, to struggle, to dispute, to quarrel
	夕	争	争	競争 *kyōsō*, competition 言い争う *ii-arasou*, to quarrel
451 **6 strokes**				争奪戦 *sōdatsusen*, scramble, contest, challenge

相	一	十	才	**SŌ**, appearance, aspect, phase; **SHŌ** (minister of state); *ai*, each other, mutual
	木	村	机	相談 *sōdan*, consultation, talk 相手 *aite*, companion, the other party
452 **9 strokes**	相	相	相	首相 *shushō*, prime minister

速	一	ニ	日	**SOKU**; *haya(i)*, speedy, quick
	申	束	束	速度 *sokudo*, speed 速記 *sokki*, stenography, short-hand
453 **10 strokes**	涑	涑	速	速達 *sokutatsu*, express mail, special delivery (口 27)

息	ノ	イ	白	**SOKU** (son); *iki*, breath
	自	自	自	ため息 *tameiki*, sigh 休息 *kyūsoku*, rest
454 **10 strokes**	息	息	息	消息 *shōsoku*, news, letter, circumstances

族	方 方 扩	ZOKU, family, tribe, clan
	扩 扩 扩	家族　*kazoku*, family, household 民族　*minzoku*, race, people, nation
455 11 strokes	扩 族 族	水族館　*suizokukan*, aquarium (方 138)

続	糸 糸 糸	ZOKU; *tsuzu(ki)*, continuation, sequel, range; *tsuzu(ku)*, to continue, to follow, to last (v.i.); *tsuzu(keru)*, to continue, to resume (v.t.)
	統 統 続	続出　*zokushutsu*, successive occurrence
456 13 strokes	続 続	手続　*tetsuzuki*, procedure 相続　*sōzoku*, inheritance (糸 83)

卒	、 亠 广	SOTSU, a private, common soldier; (to finish)
	卆 亣 交	卒業　*sotsugyō*, graduation 卒業生　*sotsugyōsei*, graduate
457 8 strokes	卆 卒	兵卒　*heisotsu*, private (soldier)

孫	⁊ 了 子	SON; *mago*, grandchild
	孑 犯 孫	子孫　*shison*, descendants
458 10 strokes	孫 孫 孫	(糸 83)

他	ノ イ 仁	TA, other
	仲 他	他国　*takoku*, other countries 他人　*tanin*, other people, stranger
459 5 strokes		その他　*sonota*, the others, the rest; and so forth

打 **460** 5 strokes	一 扌 打	十 扌	扌 打	DA; *u(tsu)*, to strike, to beat 舌打ち *shita-uchi*, smacking one's lips, click of the tongue 打者 *dasha*, batter, hitter 三塁打 *sanrui-da*, three-base hit
対 **461** 7 strokes	丶 文 対	丄 文	亍 対	TAI, opposite, against; TSUI, pair, set 反対 *hantai*, opposition, opposite, objection, reverse 対面 *taimen*, interview, confrontation 二対一 *ni-tai-ichi*, (score of) 2 to 1
隊 **462** 12 strokes	フ 阝 阼	３ 阝 隊	阝 阼 隊	TAI, a party, a corps, band, unit 兵隊 *heitai*, soldier 楽隊 *gakutai*, band (musical) 隊長 *taichō*, captain, commander, leader (豖 家 53)
代 **463** 5 strokes	ノ 代	イ 代	仁	DAI, generation, price; *ka(wari)*, substitute, deputy, compensation, exchange; *ka(waru)*, to take the place of, to relieve; *yo*, generation, the age, the reign 時代 *jidai*, period, era, age 現代 *gendai*, the present age 代表 *daihyō*, representative
題 **464** 18 strokes	日 旱 匙 趸	旦 昰 匙 趸	早 是 題	DAI, subject, topic, theme, title (of book, story, etc.) 問題 *mondai*, question, problem 話題 *wadai*, topic of conversation 宿題 *shukudai*, homework (日 11, 貝 169)

達	土	キ	ま	TATSU; *tas(suru)*, to arrive, to reach, to attain (one's object)
	ま	ま	幸	発達 *hattatsu*, development 配達 *haitatsu*, delivery 達人 *tatsujin*, an expert
465 12 strokes	幸	達	達	(土 17, ⻌ 近 195)

短	ノ	⺧	⺧	TAN (shortness, defect); *mijika(i)*, short, brief
	矢	矢	矢	短気 *tanki*, quick temper 最短 *saitan*, shortest 長短 *chōtan*, long and short, merits and demerits
466 12 strokes	短	短	短	(口 27)

談	ヽ	二	言	DAN, talk
	言	言	言	相談 *sōdan*, consultation 談話 *danwa*, conversation, talk 歓談 *kandan*, pleasant chat
467 15 strokes	談	談	談	(言 392)

治	ヽ	ヽ	⺡	CHI, JI; *osa(meru)*, to rule over
	江	治	治	政治 *seiji*, politics, administration 自治 *jichi*, self-government 治療 *chiryō*, medical treatment
468 8 strokes	治	治		

置	ヽ	⼍	罒	CHI; *o(ku)*, to put, to place
	罒	四	四	位置 *ichi*, position 置物 *okimono*, ornament (for a tokonoma) 物置 *mono-oki*, storeroom
469 13 strokes	罖	罝	置	(目 25)

| 帳 470 11 strokes | 丶 巾 帳 | 冂 帐 帳 | 巾 帐 帳 | **CHŌ** (curtain, register)
 帳面 *chōmen*, notebook, account book ┃ book
 手帳 *techō*, memo book, note-
 日記帳 *nikkichō*, diary
 (長 116) |

| 調 471 15 strokes | 言 訂 調 | 言 訂 調 | 訂 訂 | **CHŌ**; *shira(be)*, melody, inspection; *shira(beru)*, to investigate, to examine, to inspect
 調子 *chōshi*, tune, key, rhythm, tone, way, condition
 調査 *chōsa*, investigation, examination
 調節 *chōsetsu*, adjustment
 (言 392, 口 27) |

| 直 472 8 strokes | 一 有 直 | 十 有 直 | 广 直 | **CHOKU, JIKI**; *nao(su)*, to mend, to correct, to cure, to set right
 直角 *chokkaku*, right angle
 正直 *shōjiki*, honesty
 素直 *sunao*, gentle, obedient |

| 丁 473 2 strokes | 一 | 丁 | | **TEI**, " D " grade; **CHŌ**, Japanese linear unit (120 yds.), division of a ward or town, leaf of a book
 横丁 *yokochō*, side street, alleyway
 丁度 *chōdo*, exactly, just
 丁寧 *teinei*, politeness |

| 定 474 8 strokes | 丶 宀 定 | 丷 宁 定 | 广 宇 | **TEI, JŌ**; *sada(meru)*, to fix, to decide, to establish
 定員 *tei-in*, regular staff, full number of personnel
 定期 *teiki*, fixed period or term, regularity; prefix for " regular "
 予定 *yotei*, previous arrangement, program, schedule |

底 ｀ 亠 广 广 庐 庐 底 底 475 8 strokes	TEI; *soko* [*zoko*], bottom, depth 谷底　*tanizoko*, bottom of a ravine 海底　*kaitei*, bottom of the sea 徹底的　*tetteiteki*, thoroughgoing, out-and-out
停 ノ イ イ´ 伫 仁 仁 停 停 停 476 11 strokes	TEI (to stop) 停止　*teishi*, stop, suspension 停電　*teiden*, electricity stoppage 停留所　*teiryūjo*, stopping place, streetcar (bus) stop
庭 ｀ 亠 广 广 广 庄 庭 庭 庭 477 10 strokes	TEI; *niwa*, garden 庭園　*teien*, garden 校庭　*kōtei*, school playground 家庭　*katei*, home
的 ノ イ 白 白 白 白´ 的 的 478 8 strokes	TEKI (like, similar), suffix for forming adjectives from nouns; *mato*, mark, target 目的　*mokuteki*, purpose 世界的　*sekaiteki*, international, world-wide 社会的　*shakaiteki*, social
転 一 亘 亘 車 車 車一 転 転 479 1 strokes	TEN (to turn round, to change, to fall, to tumble) 転校　*tenkō*, change of schools 転任　*tennin*, change of post 運転　*unten*, driving, working, operation (車 88)

徒	⼀	⼳	⼻	**TO** (companion)
	彳	彳	待	生徒　　　*seito*, pupil, student 徒歩　　　*toho*, going on foot 徒競走　*tokyōsō*, running match
480 10 strokes	徒	徒		(土　17)

努	⼂	乂	女	**DO**; *tsuto(meru)*, to make efforts
	奴	奴	努	努力　　　*doryoku*, effort 努力家　*doryokuka*, hard worker
481 7 strokes	努			

湯	⼂	⼂	⼱	**TŌ**; *yu*, hot water
	氵日	氵旦	渂	湯気　*yuge*, steam 湯船　*yubune*, bathtub 熱湯　*nettō*, boiling water
482 12 strokes	湯	湯	湯	(日　11)

登	⼃	⼡	⺇	**TŌ, TO**; *nobo(ri)*, climbing (n.); *nobo(ru)*, to climb
	癶	癶	発	登山　　*tozan*, mountain climbing 登校　　*tōkō*, attending school 木登り　*ki-nobori*, tree climbing
483 12 strokes	咎	咎	登	(口　27)

等	⼃	⼂	⺈	**TŌ**, class, quality; *hito(shii)*, like, equal
	⺮	竹	笁	上等　　*jōtō*, high-class, very 　　　　　good, superior 一等　　*ittō*, first class, most, 　　　　　best　　　　⌈school
484 12 strokes	笁	等	等	高等学校　*kōtōgakkō*, senior high (土　17)

111

| 燈 485 16 strokes | ᠘ 灯 灯 | 火 灯 燈 | 灯 炒 燈 | **TŌ** (light, lamp) 電燈 *dentō*, electric light 安全燈 *anzentō*, safety lamp 懷中電燈 *kaichūdentō*, flashlight, electric torch (火 13, 登 483) |

| 堂 486 11 strokes | ᠊ 少 堂 | ᠍ 严 堂 | 少 当 堂 | **DŌ**, temple, hall 食堂 *shokudō*, dining room, eating house 公会堂 *kōkaidō*, town hall, public hall 国会議事堂 *Kokkai-gijidō*, the Diet Building (口 27) |

| 童 487 12 strokes | ᠍ 产 章 | 土 立 章 | 六 音 童 | **DŌ** (child) 児童 *jidō*, child, boys and girls 童話 *dōwa*, nursery tale 童謡 *dōyō*, nursery song (里 332) |

| 働 488 13 strokes | ノ 偅 働 | 亻 偅 働 | 伃 俥 | **DŌ**; *hatara(ki)*, work (n.); *hatara(ku)*, to work, to do (evil), to come into play 労働者 *rōdōsha*, laborer 働き手 *hatarakite*, bread winner, worker 「er 働き者 *hatarakimono*, hard work- (重 245) |

| 内 489 4 strokes | ᠀ 内 | 冂 | 内 | **NAI, DAI**; *uchi*, inside, home, within, during, among, between 案内 *annai*, guidance, invitation 内海 *uchiumi, naikai*, inland sea 内容 *naiyō*, contents |

熱	土	寺	夫	NETSU, heat, fever, craze, zeal; *nes(suru)*, to heat, to become hot; *atsu(i)*, hot
	垫	刲丿	执	熱病　*netsubyō*, fever 熱心　*nesshin*, zeal
490 15 strokes	執	執	執	熱帯　*nettai*, tropical zone (土　17)

農	冂	曲	曲	NŌ, farming
	曲	严	严	農場　*nōjō*, farm 農業　*nōgyō*, agriculture 農家　*nōka*, farmhouse
491 13 strokes	農	農	農	

反	一	厂	万	HAN, antithesis, anti-; TAN, unit of measure (for land and cloth)
	反			反対　*hantai*, opposition, contrast 反省　*hansei*, self-examination 反射　*hansha*, reflection
492 4 strokes				

飛	て	て	て	HI; *to(bu)*, to fly
	飞	飞	飛	飛び込む　*tobikomu*, to jump in, to dive into, to rush in 飛行機　*hikōki*, airplane
493 9 strokes	飛	飛	飛	飛行場　*hikōjō*, airport

悲	丿	丁	彐	HI; *kana(shii)*, sad
	彐	彐l	非	悲劇　*higeki*, tragedy, tragic event 悲壮　*hisō*, pathetic 慈悲　*jihi*, mercy
494 12 strokes	非	非	悲	(心　95)

113

費	一	ニ	三	HI [PI]; *tsui(yasu)*, to spend
	弓	弗	弗	費用　*hiyō*, expense 旅費　*ryohi*, traveling expenses 出費　*shuppi*, expenditure
495 12 strokes	費	費		(貝 169)

鼻	亻	宀	自	BI; *hana*, nose 鼻先　*hanasaki*, tip of one's nose, under one's very nose
	自	鳥	畠	鼻紙　*hanagami*, paper handkerchief
496 14 strokes	畠	鼻	鼻	鼻血　*hanaji*, nosebleed (田 40, 自 229)

必	`	ノ	义	HITSU; *kanara(zu)*, without fail, by all means, invariably, necessarily
	必	必		必要　*hitsuyō*, need ⌐peration 必死　*hisshi*, inevitable death, des-
497 5 strokes				必勝　*hisshō*, sure victory

氷	丿	丶	刁	HYŌ; *kōri*, ice
	氺	氷		氷すべり　*kōrisuberi*, ice skating 氷山　*hyōzan*, iceberg 砕氷船　*saihyōsen*, icebreaker
498 5 strokes				

秒	丿	二	千	BYŌ, second (unit of time)
	千	禾	利	秒針　*byōshin*, second hand 一秒　*ichibyō*, one second 数秒　*sūbyō*, several seconds
499 9 strokes	利	秒	秒	

不 500 4 strokes	一 丁	不	FU, dis-, in-, un-, mal-, ill- 不自由 *fujiyū*, inconvenience, want 「plaint 不平 *fuhei*, discontent, com- 不幸 *fukō*, misfortune, unhap- piness, death
夫 501 4 strokes	一 二 夫	夫	FU [PU], (FŪ); *otto*, husband 工夫 *kōfu*, laborer, coolie 夫婦 *fūfu*, husband and wife 夫人 *fujin*, married lady, Mrs.
付 502 5 strokes	ノ イ 付	仁 付	FU; *tsu(ku)* [*zu(ku)*], to adhere, to stick (v.i.); *tsu(keru)*, to attach, to stick (v.t.) 付近 *fukin*, neighborhood 寄付 *kifu*, contribution 受付 *uketsuke*, acceptance, infor- mation office
府 503 8 strokes	丶 亠 广 广 疒 府	庁 府	FU, urban prefecture, center 政府 *seifu*, government 首府 *shufu*, capital 府県 *fuken*, prefectures
部 504 11 strokes	丶 亠 ㄜ 音 音 部	立 音 部	BU, department, copy, part 全部 *zembu*, all, whole 東部 *tōbu*, eastern part 部分 *bubun*, part (口 27)

115

服	ノ	刀	月	FUKU, dress, European clothes
	月	肝	肝	洋服　*yōfuku*, European clothes
				礼服　*reifuku*, full dress
505 **8 strokes**	服	服		制服　*seifuku*, uniform

福	丶	ラ	ネ	FUKU, good fortune
	ネ	ネ	礻	幸福　　*kōfuku*, happiness 福の神　*fuku-no-kami*, God of Wealth
506 **13 strokes**	禣	福	福	祝福　　*shukufuku*, blessing (口　27,　田　40)

粉	゛	゛	半	FUN; *kona*, *ko*, powder
	半	米	米	火の粉　*hi-no-ko*, spark 小麦粉　*komugiko*, wheat flour
507 **10 strokes**	籵	粉	粉	製粉　　*seifun*, milling (flour)

別	丶	ロ	ロ	BETSU, distinction, exception; different, particular; *waka(reru)*, to part (from)
	号	另	別	特別　　*tokubetsu*, special 別問題　*betsumondai*, another
508 **7 strokes**	別			question 「tion 別れ　　*wakare*, parting, separa-

変	丶	亠	ナ	HEN, odd; disturbance, accident, change; *ka(waru)*, to change, to be uncommon, to move (v.i.); *ka(eru)*, to change, to reform
	六	亦	亦	変化　*henka*, change, variety, conjugation 「rible
509 **9 strokes**	亦	変	変	大変　*taihen*, serious, great, ter-

116

便 510 9 strokes	ノ イ 仁 仁 価 価 価 便 便	BEN, convenience, bodily waste; BIN, mail 便利　　*benri*, convenience 便所　　*benjo*, toilet 航空便　*kōkūbin*, air mail
包 511 5 strokes	ノ ク 勺 勺 包	HŌ; *tsutsu(mu)*, to wrap, to cover 小包　　　*kozutsumi*, postal package 包み紙　*tsutsumigami*, wrapping paper 包囲　　　*hōi*, encirclement
放 512 8 strokes	丶 亠 方 方 扩 扩 扩 放	HŌ; *hana(su)*, to let go, to release; *hana(tsu)*, to set free, to send forth, to shoot 放送　　*hōsō*, broadcasting 放課後　*hōkago*, after school 開放　　*kaihō*, freedom, opening
法 513 8 strokes	丶 冫 氵 氵 汁 汁 法 法	HŌ [PŌ], law, doctrine, reason, method 方法　　*hōhō*, way, method 法律　　*hōritsu*, law 文法　　*bumpō*, grammar
望 514 11 strokes	丶 亠 亡 亡刀 亡月 亡月 亡月 望 望	BŌ, MŌ; *nozo(mi)*, desire, wish; *nozo(mu)*, to desire, to expect, to see 失望　*shitsubō*, disappointment 希望　*kibō*, hope, wish 絶望　*zetsubō*, despair (月 12)

117

末	一	二	丰	MATSU; *sue*, end, future, youngest child, trifle
	才	末		末っ子 **suekko**, youngest child
515				月末 **getsumatsu**, end of the month
5 strokes				始末 **shimatsu**, management, circumstances

味	丶	口	口	MI; *aji*, taste, relish, experience
	口一	口二	吽	無味 **mumi**, tastelessness
				味方 **mikata**, friend, ally
516	吽	味		興味 **kyōmi**, interest, enjoyment
8 strokes				

脈	ノ	刀	月	MYAKU, pulse, hope, range
	肝	肝	肵	山脈 **sammyaku**, mountain range
				静脈 **jōmyaku**, (blood) vein
517	脈	脈	脈	鉱脈 **kōmyaku**, vein of ore
10 strokes				

民	フ	コ	コ	MIN; *tami*, people, subjects
	巨	民		市民 **shimin**, townsman
				国民 **kokumin**, nation
518				民族 **minzoku**, race
5 strokes				

命	ノ	人	合	MEI, order, command; MYŌ; *inochi*, life
	合	合	合	
				命令 **meirei**, order, command
				使命 **shimei**, mission
519	命	命		生命 **seimei**, life, soul
8 strokes				

問	丨	冂	冃
	冃	門	門
520 11 strokes	門	門	問

MON; *to(u)*, to ask, to question, to care, to accuse

問題 *mondai*, problem, issue, trouble
学問 *gakumon*, learning
疑問 *gimon*, doubt, question

(口 27)

薬	一	十	艹
	苩	苩	泊
521 16 strokes	泊	漜	薬

YAKU; *kusuri*, medicine, chemicals

薬学 *yakugaku*, pharmacy (study)
火薬 *kayaku*, gunpowder
薬局 *yakkyoku*, pharmacy, pharmacist's office

(木 15, 白 37)

油	丶	冫	氵
	氵	沪	汕
522 8 strokes	油	油	

YU; *abura*, oil

油絵 *abura-e*, oil painting
石油 *sekiyu*, petroleum
油田 *yuden*, oil field

有	ノ	ナ	广
	冇	有	有
523 6 strokes			

YŪ, U; *a(ru)*, to exist, to have, to measure, to have experience, to happen, to consist of

有名 *yūmei*, fame, well-known
有益 *yūeki*, benefit, profit
有志 *yūshi*, volunteer

勇	マ	マ	マ
	丙	丙	甬
524 9 strokes	甬	勇	勇

YŪ; *isa(mashii)*, brave

勇気 *yūki*, courage
勇士 *yūshi*, brave man
勇敢 *yūkan*, bravery

119

	マ	マ	マ	YO (previous)
予		予		予防 *yobō*, prevention
				予定 *yotei*, previous arrangement, schedule
525 4 strokes				予想 *yosō*, anticipation

	`	`	`	YŌ, ocean
洋				西洋 *seiyō*, the West, the Occident
	シ	シ	シ	洋間 *yōma*, Western-style room
526 9 strokes	洋	洋	洋	洋服 *yōfuku*, Western-style clothes

	フ	孑	阝	YŌ (positive, male principle in nature)
陽	阝日	阝旦	阝旦	太陽 *taiyō*, sun
				太陽系 *taiyōkei*, solar system
527 12 strokes	陽	陽	陽	陽気 *yōki*, season, weather, cheerfulness
				(日 11)

	ノ	二	千	RI, advantage, profit, interest (on money)
利	千	禾	利	利用 *riyō*, utilization
	利			利益 *rieki*, gains, benefit
528 7 strokes				権利 *kenri*, a right, a claim

	フ	了	阝	RIKU, land
陸	阝⁻	阝十	阝圭	大陸 *tairiku*, continent
				上陸 *jōriku*, landing
529 11 strokes	陸	陸	陸	着陸 *chakuriku*, landing (of an airplane)

良	ヽ	ゥ	∍
	∍	臼	良
530 7 strokes	良		

RYŌ; *yo(i)*, good, well, fine, right, satisfactory

改良 *kairyō*, improvement
良心 *ryōshin*, conscience
最良 *sairyō*, the best, the ideal

料	ヽ	ヽ	∨
	半	半	米
531 10 strokes	米	料	料

RYŌ (charge, materials)

原料 *genryō*, raw material
料理 *ryōri*, cooking
料金 *ryōkin*, charge

緑	糸	糸	糸
	糸	糸	絽
532 14 strokes	緑	緑	緑

RYOKU, ROKU; *midori*, green

新緑 *shinryoku*, fresh verdure
緑地 *ryokuchi*, green tract of land
緑色 *midori-iro*, green (color)

(糸 83)

輪	車	軒	軩
	軩	軩	輪
533 15 strokes	輪	輪	輪

RIN; *wa*, ring, circle, wheel

三輪車 *sanrinsha*, tricycle, three-wheeled vehicle
車輪 *sharin*, wheel
首輪 *kubiwa*, collar (for a dog)

(車 88)

類	∨	米	米
	米 ナ	米 夫	米 夫
534 18 strokes	米 夫	類	類

RUI, a kind, a variety

種類 *shurui*, kind, sort
親類 *shinrui*, a relative
分類 *bunrui*, classification

(米 135, 貝 169)

冷 535 7 strokes	丶 冫 冷	冫	冫	REI; *tsume(tai)*, cold; *hi(eru)*, to grow cold, feel chilly; *hi(yasu)*, to cool (v.t.) 冷水　*reisui*, cold water 冷気　*reiki*, cold air 冷蔵　*reizō*, cold storage, refriger-⌐ation

REI; *tsume(tai)*, cold; *hi(eru)*, to grow cold, feel chilly; *hi(yasu)*, to cool (v.t.)

冷水　*reisui*, cold water
冷気　*reiki*, cold air　　　　　⌐ation
冷蔵　*reizō*, cold storage, refriger-

REKI (to pass, to travel about)

歴史　*rekishi*, history
経歴　*keireki*, background (of a person), career
履歴書　*rirekisho*, personal history
(木 15)

536　14 strokes

RETSU, row, line

行列　*gyōretsu*, row, procession
列車　*ressha*, train
整列　*seiretsu*, standing in a row

537　6 strokes

REN, a ream (of paper), a group; ~*ren*, suffix for " group "; *tsu-(reru)*, to take along; *tsu(ranaru)*, to range; ~*zure*, suffix for " companion "

連絡　*renraku*, connection, communication, contact
連盟　*remmei*, league
(車 88)

538　10 strokes

REN; *ne(ru)*, to polish (one's style), to discipline (one's mind), to parade, to knead (a dough)

練習　*renshū*, practice
熟練　*jukuren*, skill, dexterity
訓練　*kunren*, drill, training
(糸 83)

539　14 strokes

路	ロ	口	足	RO (road, route, path); ~*ji*, suffix denoting "way"
	足	足	趵	道路 *dōro*, road 線路 *senro*, railway track 航路 *kōro*, sea route
540 13 strokes	跂	路	路	(口 27)

老	一	十	土	RŌ, old age; *o(i)*, old age, the aged; *o(iru)*, to grow old
	耂	耂	老	老人 *rōjin*, old man 老木 *rōboku*, aged tree 養老院 *yōrōin*, asylum for the aged
541 6 strokes				

労	`	``	```	RŌ, labor, service, trouble
	门	宀	学	苦労 *kurō*, toil, care 勤労 *kinrō*, labor 労働者 *rōdōsha*, laborer
542 7 strokes	労			

録	金	釒	釒	ROKU (to copy, to write down)
	釒	鈩	鈩	記録 *kiroku*, record 新記録 *shinkiroku*, new record 録音 *rokuon*, (sound) recording, transcription
543 16 strokes	鈩	録	録	

圧	一	厂	厂	ATSU (pressure)
	斤	圧		気圧 *kiatsu*, atmospheric pressure 圧力 *atsuryoku*, pressure 電圧 *den-atsu*, voltage
544 5 strokes				

易	丶	冂	日	I (easy); EKI, divination
				容易 *yōi*, easy
	日	月	易	貿易 *bōeki*, trade
				易者 *ekisha*, fortuneteller
545 8 strokes	易	易		

胃	丶	冂	冂	I, stomach
				胃袋 *ibukuro*, stomach
	罒	田	甲	胃病 *ibyō*, stomach trouble
				胃腸 *i-chō*, stomach and intestines
546 9 strokes	胃	胃	胃	

移	丿	二	千	I; *utsu(ru)*, to move (to a place, into a house), to change (v.i.), to sink into, to be infectious; *utsu-(su)*, to remove (v.t.), to infect
	千	禾	利	移民 *imin*, immigration (emigration), immigrant
547 11 strokes	秒	移	移	移り変わる *utsurikawaru*, to change, to shift

因	丨	冂	円	IN, cause; *yo(ru)*, to be due to, to be based on
	囚	因	因	原因 *gen-in*, cause
				因果 *inga*, cause and effect, fate
548 6 strokes				因襲 *inshū*, long-established custom

栄	丶	丷	丷	EI, honor; *saka(e)*, prosperity; *sa-ka(eru)*, to prosper
	灬	丷	丷	光栄 *kōei*, honor
				繁栄 *han-ei*, prosperity
549 9 strokes	栄	栄	栄	栄養 *eiyō*, nutrition

永 550 5 strokes	ヽ 永	゛ ϳ 永	ヲ ϳ	EI (long, eternal, perpetual) 永遠　*eien*, eternity 永眠　*eimin*, death 永住　*eijū*, permanent residence
衛 551 16 strokes	イ 徏 徫	イ 徉 徫	仲 徨 衛	EI (to protect, to defend) 衛生　*eisei*, hygiene 防衛　*bōei*, defense 守衛　*shuei*, guard, watchman (行 73)
液 552 11 strokes	シ 汀 液	ϳ 汁 液	氵 汸 液	EKI, liquid, fluid, juice 液体　*ekitai*, liquid 血液　*ketsueki*, blood 消毒液　*shōdoku-eki*, antiseptic solution (氵 汽 60)
演 553 14 strokes	シ 渲 演	氵 浦 演	沪 演 演	EN; *en(zuru)*, to act, to perform a play, to create (a comic scene), to commit (a blunder) 演説　*enzetsu*, speech 演技　*engi*, acting 演奏　*ensō*, (musical) performance (氵 汽 60, 宀 空 65)
央 554 5 strokes	ヽ 央	冂 央	凸	Ō (center, middle) 中央　*chūō*, center 中央線　*Chūō-sen*, the Chūō Line (electric railway in Tōkyō) 震央　*shin-ō*, the epicenter, the center of an earthquake

往	′	⁄	⼻	Ō (to go; ancient times)
	彳	行	行	往来　　 *ōrai*, (street) traffic, going and coming, street
555	往	往		往復　　 *ōfuku*, going and returning, round trip
8 strokes				立往生　 *tachi-ōjō*, standstill

応	﹀	亠	广	Ō; *ō(zuru)*, to answer, to comply with, to apply for, to accept
	広	応	応	応援　　 *ōen*, aid, cheering
556	応			応用　　 *ōyō*, practical application
7 strokes				応接間　 *ōsetsuma*, parlor

億	′	⼻	仁	OKU, one hundred million
	伶	倍	倍	二十億年　 *nijūoku-nen*, two billion years
557	億	億	億	数億円　　 *sūoku-en*, several hundred million yen
15 strokes				(立 149, 日 早 104)

恩	′	⼌	円	ON, favor, kindness
	円	内	因	恩人　　 *onjin*, benefactor
	因	恩	恩	謝恩　　 *shaon*, expression of gratitude
558	′			恩返し　 *ongaeshi*, requital of another's favor
10 strokes				(心 95)

仮	′	⼻	仁	KA, KE; *kari*, temporary, false
	仮	仮	仮	仮定　 *katei*, supposition
559				仮装　 *kasō*, disguise
6 strokes				仮病　 *kebyō*, pretended illness

果	ヽ	口	日	KA (fruit, result); *hate*, end, result; *hata(su)*, to carry out, to realize, to fulfill
	日	旦	甲	
560 8 strokes	果	果		結果 *kekka*, result, effect 効果 *kōka*, effect 果実 *kajitsu*, fruit

河	`	⁚	⁝	KA [GA] (river)
	氵	沂	沪	河口 *kakō*, mouth of a river 銀河 *ginga*, Milky Way 運河 *unga*, canal
561 8 strokes	沪	河		

過	ヽ	冂	冊	KA; *su(giru)*, to elapse, to pass, to exceed; *su(gosu)*, to pass (a day), to go to excess
	冎	咼	咼	通過 *tsūka*, passage 経過 *keika*, progress, lapse 過去 *kako*, past, past tense
562 12 strokes	咼	渦	過	(口 27, 辶 近 195)

価	ノ	イ	仁	KA; *atai*, price, value
	伝	価	価	定価 *teika*, fixed price 価値 *kachi*, value 物価 *bukka*, prices of commodities
563 8 strokes	価	価		

課	`	⁼	亖	KA, section, lesson
	言	訓	誯	課外 *kagai*, extra-curricular 課題 *kadai*, theme, homework 学課 *gakka*, lesson
564 15 strokes	誯	評	課	(言 392, 果 560)

賀	フ	カ	カロ	GA (congratulations) 年賀 *nenga*, New Year's greetings 年賀状 *nengajō*, New Year's card 祝賀 *shukuga*, celebration, congratulation
	加	智	智	
565 12 strokes	智	賀	賀	(口 27)

快	ﾉ	ｨ	忄	KAI; *kokoroyo(i)*, pleasant, refreshing 快晴 *kaisei*, fine weather 愉快 *yukai*, pleasant 快活 *kaikatsu*, cheerful
	忉	忉	忰	
566 7 strokes	快			

解	ク	角	角	KAI (explanation); *to(ku)*, to solve, to untie, to dissolve 理解 *rikai*, understanding 解散 *kaisan*, breaking up, dissolution 分解 *bunkai*, analysis, decomposi-
	角	觪	觪	
567 13 strokes	觪	解	解	⌐tion (角 173)

各	ﾉ	ク	夂	KAKU; *ono-ono*, each, every 各地 *kakuchi*, every place 各人 *kakujin*, each person 各駅 *kaku-eki*, each station
	冬	各	各	
568 6 strokes				

格	一	十	才	KAKU, status, case (in grammar) 性格 *seikaku*, personality, character 人格 *jinkaku*, character 価格 *kakaku*, price
	木	杓	杦	
569 10 strokes	格			(各 568)

確	石	石′	矿	KAKU; *tashi(ka)*, sure, accurate, reliable; *tashi(kameru)*, to ascertain, to confirm
	矿	矿	矿	正確　*seikaku*, correctness 確実　*kakujitsu*, certainty
570 15 strokes	碎	碎	確	確定　*kakutei*, decision (石 44)

完	丶	丷	宀	KAN (end, completion)
	宁	宁	宇	完全　*kanzen*, perfection 完成　*kansei*, completion 完結　*kanketsu*, completion, finish,
571 7 strokes	完			termination

漢	氵	氵	氵	KAN (China); ~*kan*, suffix for "man"
	汁	浩	浩	漢字　*kanji*, Chinese character 漢文　*kambun*, Chinese composi- 　　　　tion
572 13 strokes	澊	漢	漢	悪漢　*akkan*, villain, crook (氵 氵 60, 口 27)

管	ノ	ト	ケ	KAN (to control, to administer); *kuda*, tube, pipe
	竹	竹	竹	鉄管　*tekkan*, iron pipe (tube) 血管　*kekkan*, blood vessel 管理　*kanri*, administration, con-
573 14 strokes	管	管	管	trol, charge (官 364)

慣	丶	忄	忄	KAN; *na(reru)*, to get accustomed (to), to become inured (to)
	忄	忄ロ	忄ロ	習慣　*shūkan*, habit, custom 慣用　*kan-yō*, common use, 　　　　practice
574 14 strokes	忄罒	慣	慣	見慣れる　*minareru*, to get used to 　　　　seeing, to be familiar 　　　　(with) (貝 169)

希 **575** 7 strokes	ノ 孚 希	メ 孚	メ 希	**KI** (rare; desire) 希望 *kibō*, hope, desire 希望者 *kibōsha*, aspirant, applicant 希薄 *kihaku*, thin, weak, sparse
寄 **576** 11 strokes	丶 宀 宔	丶 宇 害	宀 宨 寄	**KI**; *yo(ru)*, to approach, to drop in, to gather (v. i.); *yo(seru)*, to draw up (a chair), to push (a desk) aside 寄港 *kikō*, call at a port 寄付 *kifu*, contribution 寄与 *kiyo*, contribution, service (口 27)
規 **577** 11 strokes	一 夫 担	二 扣 捍	丰 担 規	**KI** (compass) 規律 *kiritsu*, order, discipline 規模 *kibo*, scale, scope 規準 *kijun*, standard (見 67)
紀 **578** 9 strokes	く 糸 紀	幺 糸 紀	幺 糸 紀	**KI** (history, chronicle) 世紀 *seiki*, century, period 二十世紀 *nijisseiki*, twentieth century 紀元 *kigen*, era, epoch
技 **579** 7 strokes	一 扌 技	十 扩	才 technics 抟	**GI** (art, skill) 技師 *gishi*, engineer 競技 *kyōgi*, sporting events, contest 技術 *gijutsu*, art, technique

130

義	`	`丷`	`⺍`	GI, justice, morality, loyalty, relationship; prefix for "in-law," "artificial"
	乂	乂	羊	主義 *shugi*, principle, ~ism 講義 *kōgi*, lecture
580 13 strokes	羊	莠	義	義兄 *gikei*, elder brother-in-law (我 745)

議	言	訁丷	訁⺍	GI (discussion)
	詳	詳	詳	会議 *kaigi*, conference 議論 *giron*, argument, discussion 議会 *gikai*, Diet
581 20 strokes	議			(言 392, 義 580)

久	ノ	ク	久	KYŪ, KU; *hisa(shii)*, long (time), lasting; *hisa(shiku)*, for a long time
				永久 *eikyū*, permanence, eternity ⌐time
582 3 strokes				久しぶり *hisashiburi*, after a long 久遠 *kuon*, eternity

求	一	十	寸	KYŪ; *moto(me)*, request, demand; *moto(meru)*, to request, to search for, to buy, to wish for
	汁	求	求	求人 *kyūjin*, offer of a job
583 7 strokes	求			請求 *seikyū*, demand ⌐ment 求職 *kyūshoku*, seeking employ-

救	一	十	寸	KYŪ; *suku(i)*, rescue, help; *suku(u)*, to rescue, to help
	求	求	求	救済 *kyūsai*, relief 救助 *kyūjo*, rescue
584 11 strokes	求	扩	救	救急車 *kyūkyūsha*, ambulance (求 583)

131

給 585 12 strokes	⟨ ⟨ ⟨ 幺 纟 糹 糸 紿 紒 給	KYŪ (to supply) 給料 *kyūryō*, pay, salary 供給 *kyōkyū*, supply 月給 *gekkyū*, monthly salary (合 77)
居 586 8 strokes	⟩ ⟩ 尸 尸 厇 斥 居 居	KYO (dwelling place); *i(ru)*, to be, to be present, to dwell 住居 *jūkyo*, dwelling 居眠り *inemuri*, napping, dozing (n.) 居間 *ima*, living room
許 587 11 strokes	⟨ ⟨ ⟨ 言 言 言 許 許 許	KYO; *yuru(shi)*, permission, pardon, approval; *yuru(su)*, to permit, to forgive, to approve 許可 *kyoka*, permission, license, admission, approval 特許 *tokkyo*, patent, concession 免許 *menkyo*, license, certificate (口 27)
漁 588 14 strokes	⟨ ⟨ ⟨ 沪 漁 漁 漁 漁 漁	GYO; RYŌ, fishing 漁船 *gyosen*, fishing boat 漁業 *gyogyō*, fishing industry 漁師 *ryōshi*, fisherman (氵 汽 60, 田 40)
興 589 16 strokes	⟨ ⟨ ⟨ 同 同 同 興 興 興	KYŌ, interest; KŌ; *oko(ru)*, to prosper; *oko(su)*, to restore 興味 *kyōmi*, interest, appeal 興奮 *kōfun*, excitement 復興 *fukkō*, revival, reconstruction (同 295)

均	一	十	土	KIN (level, equality)
	圩	圴	坾	平均 *heikin*, average, balance
590	均			均等 *kintō*, equality, identity
7 strokes				

区	一	丆	又	KU, ward, section
	区			区別 *kubetsu*, distinction, classification
591				地区 *chiku*, area
4 strokes				区画 *kukaku*, boundary, block, division

句	ノ	勹	勹	KU, clause, phrase, verse, line
	句	句		文句 *monku*, words, objection
592				語句 *goku*, words and phrases
5 strokes				句とう点 *kutōten*, punctuation marks

軍	ノ	冖	冖	GUN, army, military authorities
	冖	冒	冒	軍備 *gumbi*, armaments
593	冒	宣	軍	軍隊 *guntai*, troops, army
9 strokes				軍艦 *gunkan*, warship

群	ヨ	尹	君	GUN; *mu(re)*, group, flock, herd; *mu(reru)*, *mura(garu)*, to throng (v. i.)
	君	君	君	魚群 *gyogun*, school of fish
594	群	群	群	群島 *guntō*, group of islands
13 strokes				群衆 *gunshū*, crowd (of people)
				(君 198)

133

型	一	二	干	KEI; *kata* [*gata*], type, model, mold, conventionality
	开	刑	刑	模型 *mokei*, model 小型 *kogata*, small size 大型 *ō-gata*, large size
595 9 strokes	型	型	型	

経	く	纟	幺	KEI, circles of longitude; KYŌ, the sutras, (law, reason, way, ordinary course of things); *he(ru)*, to pass, to pass through
	糸	糸	糸	経費 *keihi*, expenditure 経由 *keiyu*, by way of, through 神経 *shinkei*, nerve
596 11 strokes	紀	経	経	(土 17)

欠	ノ	上	ク	KETSU (lack, absence); *ka(keru)*, to be broken off, to lack (v.i.); *ka-(ku)*, to lack, to want (v.t.)
	欠			欠点 *ketten*, fault 欠席 *kesseki*, absence 欠乏 *ketsubō*, shortage
597 4 strokes				

件	ノ	亻	仴	KEN, matter
	仁	仁	件	事件 *jiken*, event, matter 用件 *yōken*, business 条件 *jōken*, condition, terms
598 6 strokes				

健	亻	亻ヿ	仴	KEN; *suko(yaka)*, healthy, sound
	仴	伊	伊	強健 *kyōken*, robust 保健 *hoken*, (preservation of) health
599 11 strokes	律	健	健	健全 *kenzen*, healthy, sound (亻 休 61)

験	丨	厂	丌
	馬	馬	馬
600 18 strokes	駖	験	験

KEN (effect; to examine)

実験 *jikken*, experiment

経験 *keiken*, experience

試験 *shiken*, examination, experiment

(馬 127, 僉 険 770)

限	フ	３	阝
	阝フ	阝ヨ	阝ヨ
601 9 strokes	阻	限	限

GEN; *kagi(ri)*, limit, end, as far as possible; *kagi(ru)*, to limit, to restrict

制限 *seigen*, limitation

期限 *kigen*, term

無限 *mugen*, infinity

現	一	丁	王
	王	玑	玥
602 11 strokes	玥	現	現

GEN (present, now); *ara(wareru)*, to show oneself, to come into sight, to be found (out); *ara(wasu)*, to manifest, to expose, to express

実現 *jitsugen*, realization

表現 *hyōgen*, expression

現代 *gendai*, present age

(見 67)

個	丿	亻	亻
	们	佰	佰
603 10 strokes	個	個	

KO (individual), suffix for enumeration

個人 *kojin*, individual

個性 *kosei*, individual character, personality

数個 *sūko*, several

(口 27)

護	言	言	許
	計	許	許
604 20 strokes	謹	護	護

GO (to protect, to defend)

保護 *hogo*, protection

看護婦 *kangofu*, trained nurse

弁護士 *bengoshi*, lawyer

(言 392, 蒦 集 243)

135

功	一	T	工	**KŌ**, merits, effect, service; **KU**
	工フ	功		成功　*seikō*, success 功績　*kōseki*, meritorious deed 功労　*kōrō*, services
605 5 strokes				

厚	一	厂	厂	**KŌ**; *atsu(i)*, thick, cordial
	厈	戸	盾	厚紙　*atsugami*, thick paper, cardboard 厚意　*kōi*, kindness 厚生　*kōsei*, public welfare
606 9 strokes	厚	厚	厚	

候	ノ	イ	亻	**KŌ**, season, (sign; to inquire after)
	亻	仁	佇	気候　*kikō*, climate, weather 天候　*tenkō*, weather 候補　*kōho*, candidacy, candidate
607 10 strokes	佐	候	候	

康	丶	亠	广	**KŌ** (to enjoy)
	庁	庐	序	健康　*kenkō*, health, good health 不健康　*fukenkō*, bad health
608 11 strokes	序	康	康	

講	言	言	訐	**KŌ** (investigation, lecture; to think out, to study, to explain)
	詳	講	講	講演　*kōen*, lecture 講堂　*kōdō*, auditorium 講習　*kōshū*, short training course
609 17 strokes	講	講	講	(言 392)

鉱	ハ	牟	金	KŌ (ore)
	金	金`	釘	鉱山　*kōzan*, mine 鉱物　*kōbutsu*, mineral 鉄鉱　*tekkō*, iron ore
610 13 strokes	釘	鉱	鉱	(金 16)

査	一	十	才	SA (to examine, to investigate)
	木	杏	杏	検査　*kensa*, inspection, examination 巡査　*junsa*, policeman 審査　*shinsa*, screening
611 9 strokes	杳	查	査	

際	⁊	⁊	阝	SAI, occasion 実際　*jissai*, actual state, truth, reality
	阝	阝	阞	国際　*kokusai*, international 交際　*kōsai*, intercourse, acquaintance, association
612 14 strokes	際	際	際	(祭 400)

在	一	ナ	才	ZAI, country, suburbs, (to exist)
	右	在	在	存在　*sonzai*, existence, being 滞在　*taizai*, sojourn 現在　*genzai*, present time, present tense
613 6 strokes				

殺	ノ	メ	メ	SATSU, SAI; *koro(su)*, to kill
	羊	羊	羊	殺人　　*satsujin*, homicide, murder 殺風景　*sappūkei*, tasteless, dreary 自殺　　*jisatsu*, suicide
614 10 strokes	剎	殺	殺	(又 収 631)

137

雑	ノ	九	九
	杂	新	新
615 14 strokes	新	雑	雑

ZATSU, rough; ZŌ (miscellaneous, rough)

複雑　*fukuzatsu*, complexity, complication

雑誌　*zasshi*, magazine

雑きん　*zōkin*, floorcloth, mopping cloth

(木 15)

参	ム	ム	ム
	参	失	矢
616 8 strokes	参	参	

SAN, three (used in legal papers); *mai(ru)*, to go, to come, to surrender, to be nonplussed, to visit for worship

参加　*sanka*, participation

参観　*sankan*, visit

参考書　*sankōsho*, reference book

蚕	一	二	ヂ
	天	天	吞
617 10 strokes	吞	蚕	蚕

SAN; *kaiko*, silkworm

養蚕　*yōsan*, sericulture

蚕室　*sanshitsu*, silkworm rearing room 「district

養蚕地　*yōsanchi*, silkworm raising

(口 27)

酸	一	酉	酌
	酌	酌	酸
618 14 strokes	酸	酸	酸

SAN, acid

酸素　*sanso*, oxygen

塩酸　*ensan*, hydrochloric acid

酸化　*sanka*, oxidization

賛	一	二	丰
	夫	麸	替
619 15 strokes	替	賛	賛

SAN (to praise, to assist, to agree)

賛成　*sansei*, approval, support

賛助　*sanjo*, support, help

協賛　*kyōsan*, cooperation

(貝 169)

氏 620 4 strokes	ノ 氏	㇄	㇗	SHI, Mister (used as suffix); *uji*, family name, lineage 氏名 *shimei*, full name 氏族制度 *shizoku-seido*, the clan or the family system 諸氏 *shoshi*, Messrs., gentlemen
支 621 4 strokes	一 支	十	方	SHI (branch; to branch off, to support) 支配 *shihai*, rule, management 支払う *shiharau*, to pay 支店 *shiten*, a branch (store, office)
示 622 5 strokes	一 示	二 示	丁	SHI, JI; *shime(su)*, to show, to point out 示唆 *shisa*, suggestion 掲示 *keiji*, notice 指示 *shiji*, instructions, indication
志 623 7 strokes	一 士 志	十 志	士 志	SHI; *kokorozashi*, will, intention, ambition, aim, kindness; *kokoro-za(su)*, to intend, to aim at 意志 *ishi*, will 志望 *shibō*, desire 同志 *dōshi*, comrade
師 624 10 strokes	ノ 𠂤 師	亻 𠂤 師	厂 𠂤 師	SHI, teacher, expert; army 牧師 *bokushi*, pastor 教師 *kyōshi*, teacher 師団 *shidan*, division (army)

似	ノ	イ	仂	JI; *ni(ru)*, to resemble
	似	似	似	類似 *ruiji*, similarity 似顔 *nigao*, portrait, likeness 不似合 *funiai*, unbecoming
625 7 strokes	似			

辞	ノ	ニ	千	JI, word, speech; *ji(suru)*, to re-sign, to take one's leave, to decline
	舌	舌丿	舌亠	辞書 *jisho*, dictionary 辞職 *jishoku*, resignation 祝辞 *shukuji*, congratulatory ad-dress
626 13 strokes	辞	辞	辞	(口 27, 立 149)

識	言	計	計	SHIKI (to know, to write down, to distinguish)
	詳	謙	譜	知識 *chishiki*, knowledge 標識 *hyōshiki*, mark 常識 *jōshiki*, common sense
627 19 strokes	識	識	識	(言 392, 日 11)

質	ノ	イ	厂	SHITSU, quality, substance, (to inquire; simple and honest); SHICHI, pawn
	斤	所	所	質問 *shitsumon*, question 素質 *soshitsu*, makings, quality 質屋 *shichiya*, pawnshop
628 15 strokes	質	質	質	(貝 169)

舍	ノ	人	合	SHA (house, lodging)
	仐	全	全	校舎 *kōsha*, school building 牛舎 *gyūsha*, cowshed 宿舎 *shukusha*, lodging
629 8 strokes	舍	舍		

謝 630 17 strokes	言	言	言
	訂	訓	訓
	誹	謝	謝

SHA; *sha(suru)*, to apologize, to thank

感謝　*kansha*, thanks
謝絶　*shazetsu*, refusal
謝礼　*sharei*, remuneration, thanks
(言 392, 身 255)

収 631 4 strokes	丨	丩	収
	収		

SHŪ; *osa(meru)*, to obtain, to pay (taxes), to accept, to store, to seize

収穫　*shūkaku*, harvest
収容　*shūyō*, admission, accommodation
収入　*shūnyū*, income

周 632 8 strokes	丿	冂	冂
	円	用	周
	周	周	

SHŪ (circumference; to go round)

周囲　*shūi*, circumference, surroundings
周辺　*shūhen*, outskirts
一周　*isshū*, one round

修 633 10 strokes	丿	亻	亻
	仈	修	修
	修	修	修

SHU, SHU; *osa(meru)*, to study, to finish, to practice

修理　*shūri*, repair
改修　*kaishū*, improvement, repair
修正　*shūsei*, amendment

宿 634 11 strokes	丶	宀	宀
	宀	宁	宁
	宿	宿	宿

SHUKU; *yado*, inn; *yado(ru)*, to lodge at

宿屋　*yadoya*, inn
宿題　*shukudai*, homework
下宿　*geshuku*, boardinghouse
(日 11)

祝	`	ラ	ネ	SHUKU; *iwa(i)*, celebration; *iwa-(u)*, to celebrate
	ネ	ネ	ネ刀	祝賀 *shukuga*, celebration
635 9 strokes	ネ刀	祀	祝	祝福 *shukufuku*, blessing 祝日 *shukujitsu*, festival day

術	ゝ	彳	行	JUTSU, art, artifice, means, magic
	什	袮	休	手術 *shujutsu*, surgical operation 技術 *gijutsu*, technique 美術 *bijutsu*, art
636 11 strokes	術	術二	術	(行 73)

準	シ	シ	氵	JUN (water level; rule; to imitate); prefix denoting "semi-," "associate"
	氵'	汾	泮	標準 *hyōjun*, standard 基準 *kijun*, standard
637 13 strokes	淮	進	準	準急 *junkyū*, semi-express (氵 汽 60, 隹 集 243)

序	`	亠	广	JO, preface
	戶	序	序	順序 *junjo*, order, method 秩序 *chitsujo*, public order, discipline
638 7 strokes	序			序文 *jobun*, preface

承	⁊	了	孑	SHŌ; *uketamawa(ru)*, to hear
	手	手	净	承知 *shōchi*, consent, knowledge 承認 *shōnin*, approval
639 8 strokes	承	承		了承 *ryōshō*, acknowledgment

省 640 9 strokes	⼂ ⼩ ⼩ ⼩ 省 省	⼃ ⼩ ⼩ ⼩ 省 省	⼩ ⼩ 省 省 省	SHŌ, suffix for "government department"; SEI (to look); *habu-(ku)*, to omit, to cut down; *kaeri-(miru)*, to reflect upon (oneself) 省略 *shōryaku*, omission 外務省 *Gaimushō*, Ministry of Foreign Affairs (Japan) 反省 *hansei*, self-examination
賞 641 15 strokes	⼂ ⺍ 嘗 賞	⼃ ⼍ 賞 賞	⺍ 常 賞 賞	SHŌ, prize 賞品 *shōhin*, prize (thing) 賞金 *shōkin*, prize (money) 鑑賞 *kanshō*, appreciation (口 27, 貝 169)
常 642 11 strokes	⼂ ⺍ 尚	⼃ ⼍ 常	⺍ 尚 常	JŌ; *tsune*, usual, ordinary 非常に *hijō-ni*, very (much) 正常 *seijō*, normal 日常 *nichijō*, everyday (口 27)
情 643 11 strokes	⼂ 忄 忄 情	⼆ 忄 忄 情	忄 忄 情 情	JŌ, feeling, sympathy; *nasa(ke)*, feeling, sympathy, love, mercy 愛情 *aijō*, affection 情け深い *nasakebukai*, compassionate 情勢 *jōsei*, state of things (月 12)
織 644 18 strokes	糸 紵 紵 織	紵 紵 織 織	紵 綞 織 織	SHOKU, SHIKI; *ori*, textile; *o(ru)*, to weave 織物 *orimono*, textile fabric 織機 *shokki*, weaving machine 組織 *soshiki*, organization (糸 83, 日 11)

				SEI, sex, nature; SHŌ, nature, temperament
性	丶	八	忄	
	忄	忄	忄	性質 *seishitsu*, nature, property 習性 *shūsei*, habit 気性 *kishō*, temper
645 8 strokes	忄	性		

				SEI, SHŌ; *matsurigoto*, government
政	一	丁	下	
	正	正	正	政府 *seifu*, government 政治 *seiji*, administration, politics 政策 *seisaku*, policy
646 9 strokes	正	政	政	

				SEI, spirit, vitality, essence; SHŌ
精	丷	丷	半	
	米	米	米	精神 *seishin*, spirit, mind, soul 精巧 *seikō*, exquisite (workmanship) 精進 *shōjin*, diligence
647 14 strokes	精	精	精	(米 135, 青 36)

				SEI (to manufacture), suffix for "make" or "manufacture"
製	丶	一	仁	製品 *seihin*, manufactured goods
	与	制	制	銀製 *ginsei*, made of silver 米国製 *Beikokusei*, of American make
648 14 strokes	制	製	製	(制 823, 衣 341)

				SEKI; *se(meru)*, to blame, to urge, to torture
責	一	十	主	
	主	青	青	責任 *sekinin*, responsibility 責任者 *sekininsha*, person responsible 無責任 *musekinin*, irresponsibility
649 11 strokes	青	責	責	(貝 169)

144

績	く	幺	糸
	糸	糸⁻	糸丰
650 **17 strokes**	糸丰	績	績

SEKI (to spin; meritorious deed)

成績　*seiseki*, result, record

功績　*kōseki*, meritorious deeds

紡績　*bōseki*, spinning

(糸 83, 貝 169)

折	一	十	扌
	扩	折	折
651 **7 strokes**	折		

SETSU; *o(ru)*, to break, to fold, to bend

曲折　*kyokusetsu*, winding, complications

折合　*oriai*, mutual relations, compromise

折り目　*orime*, crease

接	扌	扩	扩
	扩	护	拉
652 **11 strokes**	接	接	接

SETSU; *ses(suru)*, to come in contact with, to receive, to adjoin

直接　*chokusetsu*, directly

接待　*settai*, reception

接続　*setsuzoku*, junction

(扌 折 651)

設	、	二	言
	言	言	言)
653 **11 strokes**	訊	設	設

SETSU; *mō(keru)*, to establish

設備　*setsubi*, equipment

設計　*sekkei*, plan, design (for construction)

建設　*kensetsu*, construction

(言 392)

説	二	言	言
	言	訓	詳
654 **14 strokes**	詳	説	

SETSU, opinion, theory; ZEI; *to(ku)*, to explain, to persuade, to preach

説明　*setsumei*, explanation

伝説　*densetsu*, legend

社説　*shasetsu*, editorial

(口 27)

145

浅 655 9 strokes	`	`	`	SEN; *asa(i)*, shallow 浅見　*senken*, superficial view 浅薄　*sempaku*, superficial 遠浅　*tōasa*, shoaling beach, shallowness extending far from shore

銭 656 14 strokes	ノ	人	今	SEN, former unit of money (a hundredth part of a yen); *zeni*, money 金銭　　　*kinsen*, money こづかい銭　*kozukaisen*, pocket money (戔 浅 655)

祖 657 9 strokes	`	ラ	ネ	SO [ZO], ancestor, founder 祖国　*sokoku*, fatherland 祖母　*sobo*, grandmother 先祖　*senzo*, ancestor

素 658 10 strokes	一	十	圭	SO, SU (white, origin, source) 素ぼく　*soboku*, simple 要素　*yōso*, element, important factor 素顔　*sugao*, unpainted face

倉 659 10 strokes	ノ	人	스	SŌ; *kura*, warehouse 倉庫　*sōko*, warehouse 船倉　*sensō*, hold (of a ship) 米倉　*komegura*, rice granary (口 27)

146

想 660 13 strokes	一 十 才 木 机 相 相 想 想	SŌ, idea, thought 想像　*sōzō*, imagination 理想　*risō*, ideal 予想　*yosō*, expectation (目 25, 心 95)
総 661 14 strokes	く 幺 糸 紅 紛 紛 絵 総 総	SŌ (whole, general) 総理大臣　*sōri-daijin*, prime minister 総員　*sōin*, entire staff, all hands, full force 総選挙　*sōsenkyo*, general election (糸 83, 心 95)
造 662 10 strokes	ノ ヒ 屮 生 牛 告 告 造 造	ZŌ; *tsuku(ri)*, structure, build (n.); *tsuku(ru)*, to make, to create, to build; ~*zuku(ri)*, made of ~ (suffix denoting type of structure) 木造　*mokuzō*, made of wood 人造　*jinzō*, artificial 石造り　*ishizukuri*, built of stone (口 27)
象 663 12 strokes	ノ ク 夕 色 色 免 免 象 象	ZŌ, elephant; SHŌ (image) 対象　*taishō*, object 印象　*inshō*, impression 象げ　*zōge*, ivory
像 664 14 strokes	ノ イ イ 伊 伊 伊 伊 像 像	ZŌ, image, figure 銅像　*dōzō*, bronze statue 仏像　*butsuzō*, image of Buddha 現像　*genzō*, development (of a film)

147

増 665 14 strokes	一	十	土	ZŌ; ma(su), to increase (v. i. & v. t.) 増加 zōka, increase 増強 zōkyō, reinforcement 増進 zōshin, promotion (田 40, 日 11)
	圵	圵	圴	
	圴	増	増	

則 666 9 strokes	丨	冂	月	SOKU (law; to act on) 法則 hōsoku, law 規則 kisoku, rule 原則 gensoku, principle
	月	目	貝	
	貝	則	則	

側 667 11 strokes	丿	亻	仃	SOKU; kawa [gawa], side 内側 uchigawa, the inside 右側 migigawa, usoku, right side 側面 sokumen, the side
	仴	仴	俱	
	俱	側	側	

測 668 12 strokes	丶	冫	氵	SOKU; haka(ru), to fathom, to measure 観測 kansoku, observation 測量 sokuryō, surveying 測定 sokutei, measurement
	氿	泪	沮	
	測	測	測	

帯 669 10 strokes	一	十	卅	TAI; obi, girdle; o(biru), to wear 地帯 chitai, zone 熱帯 nettai, torrid zone, tropics 帯封 obifū, half wrapper
	卅	卅	带	
	带	带	帯	

148

貸 ノ イ 仁 代 代 代 貸 貸 貸 670 12 strokes	TAI; ka(shi), loan; ka(su), to lend, to loan, to hire out
	貸家 　　　kashiya, house for rent 貸ボート　　kashibōto, boat for hire 貸借 　　　taishaku, borrowing and lending

単 丶 䒑 ツ 䒑 䒑 当 単 671 9 strokes	TAN (single)
	単純　tanjun, simple 簡単　kantan, simple, easy 単価　tanka, unit price

団 丨 冂 冂 团 団 団 672 6 strokes	DAN, association; ~dan, suffix for "troupe" or "company"
	団体　dantai, party, organization 楽団　gakudan, band (musical) 団結　danketsu, unity

築 𥫗 𥫗 𥫗 𥫗 𥫗 筑 筑 筑 築 673 16 strokes	CHIKU; kizu(ku), to build
	建築　kenchiku, building 築造　chikuzō, construction 新築　shinchiku, new building (竹 113, 木 15)

貯 冂 目 貝 貝 貝丶 貝丶 貯 貯 貯 674 12 strokes	CHO (to store, to save)
	貯水池　chosuichi, reservoir 貯蔵　　chozō, storage 貯金　　chokin, savings (貝 169)

149

張	▔	⊐	弓
	引	纩	弫
675 11 strokes	弫	張	張

CHŌ; *ha(ri)* [*pa(ri)*, *ba(ri)*], tension, expansion; *ha(ru)*, to stretch, to spread, to cover
見張り   *mihari*, lookout
引っ張る   *hipparu*, to pull
主張   *shuchō*, insistence, opinion
(長 116)

腸	)	几	月
	肝	肥	肥
676 13 strokes	朡	腸	腸

CHŌ, the intestines
盲腸   *mōchō*, (vermiform) appendix
大腸   *daichō*, large intestine
腸カタル   *chōkataru*, intestinal catarrh
(月 12, 日 11)

低	ノ	イ	仁
	仟	仟	低
677 7 strokes	低		

TEI; *hiku(i)*, low, short
低気圧   *tei-kiatsu*, low atmospheric pressure
低空   *teikū*, low altitude
低地   *teichi*, low ground

敵	立	产	育
	商	商	商
678 15 strokes	啇	敵	敵

TEKI, enemy, opponent
強敵   *kyōteki*, formidable enemy
敵意   *teki-i*, hostile feeling
敵国   *tekikoku*, enemy country

適	`	亠	亠
	产	商	商
679 14 strokes	商	商	適

TEKI; *teki(suru)*, to be fit for
適当   *tekitō*, suitable, moderate
適任   *tekinin*, fitness
快適   *kaiteki*, agreeable
(辶 近 195)

150

典	丶	冂	冉	**TEN** (ceremony, celebration)
	冊	曲	曲	辞典　*jiten*, dictionary
680	典	典		古典　*koten*, classics
8 strokes				祭典　*saiten*, festival, rite

伝	丿	亻	仁	**DEN**; *tsuta(eru)*, to report, to impart, to transmit; *tsuta(waru)*, to be reported (imparted, transmitted)
	仁	伝	伝	伝記　*denki*, biography
681				伝染病　*densembyō*, epidemic
6 strokes				宣伝　*senden*, propaganda

統	く	幺	糸	**TŌ**; *su(beru)*, to control
	糸	紅	紆	統計　*tōkei*, statistics
	絵	紵	統	大統領　*daitōryō*, president (of a country)
682				伝統　*dentō*, tradition
12 strokes				(糸 83)

銅	人	合	全	**DŌ**, copper
	全	金	釗	青銅　*seidō*, bronze
	釘	銅	銅	銅線　*dōsen*, copper wire
683				銅山　*dōzan*, copper mine
14 strokes				(金 16, 冂 27)

導	丶	丷	丷	**DŌ**; *michibi(ki)*, guidance; *michibi(ku)*, to guide, to lead
	艹	首	道	指導　*shidō*, guidance
	道	導	導	指導者　*shidōsha*, leader
684				補導　*hodō*, guidance
15 strokes				(目 25, 辶 近 195)

特	丿	二	牛
	牛	牛	牡
685 10 strokes	牯	特	特

TOKU (special)

特別　*tokubetsu*, special, particular
特長　*tokuchō*, strong point
特急　*tokkyū*, limited express

(土　17)

毒	一	十	主
	主	责	责
686 8 strokes	责	毒	

DOKU, poison

気の毒　*ki-no-doku*, sorry, pitiful
毒草　*dokusō*, poisonous herb
中毒　*chūdoku*, poisoning

独	丿	犭	犭
	犭	犭	狛
687 9 strokes	狆	独	独

DOKU (one person; Germany)

独立　*dokuritsu*, independence
独特　*dokutoku*, peculiar, unique
独唱　*dokushō*, vocal solo

任	丿	亻	亻
	仁	任	任
688 6 strokes			

NIN, duty; *maka(seru)*, to entrust, to leave (v. t.)

責任　*sekinin*, responsibility
転任　*tennin*, change of post
任務　*nimmu*, duty

念	丿	人	今
	今	今	念
689 8 strokes	念	念	

NEN, thought, feeling, desire

記念　*kinen*, commemoration
残念　*zannen*, regret, disappointment
念願　*nengan*, one's heart's desire

燃	、	゛	ゾ
	火	炒	炒
690 16 strokes	炒	炒	燃

NEN; *mo(eru)*, to burn (v. i.); *mo(yasu)*, to burn (v. t.)

燃料　*nenryō*, fuel
燃焼　*nenshō*, combustion
不燃性　*funensei*, incombustible

(然 450)

能	ム	ム	ム
	台	台	肖
691 10 strokes	自'	能	能

NŌ, ability, the *Noh*

能力　*nōryoku*, ability, capacity, faculty
才能　*sainō*, talent
能率　*nōritsu*, efficiency

破	一	厂	不
	石	矴	矴
692 10 strokes	矴	破	破

HA [PA]; *yabu(re)*, a tear (rent); *yabu(ru)*, to tear, to break (a promise)

破損　*hason*, breakdown
破産　*hasan*, bankruptcy
難破　*nampa*, shipwreck

敗	丨	冂	目
	貝	貝	貝
693 11 strokes	貯	敗	敗

HAI [PAI]; *yabu(reru)*, to be defeated

敗戦　*haisen*, lost battle
腐敗　*fuhai*, putrefaction, corrup-
失敗　*shippai*, failure ⌐tion

(貝 169)

倍	ノ	イ	イ
	仁	伫	位
694 10 strokes	位	倍	倍

BAI, two times, double; suffix denoting "times"

数倍　*sūbai*, several times
何倍　*nambai*, how many times?
倍率　*bairitsu*, magnifying power

(亻 27)

博 695 12 strokes	一 十 十 十百 十甫 十甫 博 博	**HAKU** (learned; to spread; abundant) 博士　*hakushi*, doctor (degree) 博物館　*hakubutsukan*, museum 博覧会　*hakurankai*, exposition (専 830)
飯 696 12 strokes	ノ 今 今 食 食 食 飣 飯 飯	**HAN**; *meshi*, boiled rice, a meal 朝飯　*asahan*, *asameshi*, breakfast 昼飯　*hirumeshi*, lunch 夕飯　*yūhan*, *yūmeshi*, supper (食 253)
比 697 4 strokes	一 ヒ ヒ 比	**HI**, ratio, comparison; *kura(beru)*, to compare 比較　*hikaku*, comparison 比率　*hiritsu*, ratio 比例　*hirei*, proportion
非 698 8 strokes	ノ フ ヺ ヺ 非 非 非 非	**HI**, fault, wrong; non-, un- 非常に　*hijō-ni*, very 非常口　*hijōguchi*, emergency door 非難　*hinan*, censure
肥 699 8 strokes	ノ 几 月 月 肥 肥 肥 肥	**HI**; *ko(eru)*, to grow fat; *ko(yasu)*, to fertilize, to fatten, to enrich (oneself) 肥料　*hiryō*, manure, fertilizer たい肥　*taihi*, compost

154

備 700 12 strokes	ノ 什 伊	イ 什 備	仁 供 備	BI; *sona(e)*, preparation(s); *sona-(eru)*, to furnish, to prepare; *sona-(waru)*, to be possessed of, to be furnished with 準備 *jumbi*, preparation(s) 守備 *shubi*, defense 予備 *yobi*, reserve (用 146)
筆 701 12 strokes	ノ 竹 筝	ト 竺 筆	キ 竺 筆	HITSU [PITSU]; *fude*, writing brush 万年筆 *mannenhitsu*, fountain pen 鉛筆 *empitsu*, pencil 筆者 *hissha*, writer
俵 702 10 strokes	ノ 什 俵	イ 佳 俵	仁 俵 俵	HYŌ [BYŌ, PYŌ]; *tawara [da-wara]*, straw bag 土俵 *dohyō*, sandbag; sumō (wrestling) ring 一俵 *ippyō*, one straw bag 炭俵 *sumidawara*, charcoal sack
票 703 11 strokes	一 西 覀	丆 丙 票	両 西 票	HYŌ [PYŌ], vote 投票 *tōhyō*, voting 伝票 *dempyō*, chit 五十票 *gojippyō*, fifty votes (示 622)
標 704 15 strokes	一 朴 標	十 柙 標	才 標 標	HYŌ (mark, sign; to write down, to express) 標本 *hyōhon*, specimen 標語 *hyōgo*, motto 目標 *mokuhyō*, mark, object

貧	ノ	八	今	**HIN**, poverty; **BIN**; *mazu(shii)*, poor
	分	贫	贫	貧弱 *hinjaku*, meager, poor 貧乏 *bimbō*, poverty 貧困 *hinkon*, poverty, lack
705 11 strokes	貧	貧	貧	(貝 169)

布	ノ	ナ	right	**FU** [PU]; *nuno*, cloth
	右	布		毛布 *mōfu*, blanket 配布 *haifu*, distribution 綿布 *mempu*, cotton cloth
706 5 strokes				

婦	〈	女	女	**FU** (woman, wife)
	女	女ヨ	女ヨ	婦人 *fujin*, woman 主婦 *shufu*, housewife 夫婦 *fūfu*, husband and wife
707 11 strokes	婦	婦	婦	(女 32)

武	一	二	三	**BU, MU**, military
	干	正	正	武装 *busō*, arms, weapons 武器 *buki*, weapon 武力 *buryoku*, military power
708 8 strokes	武	武		

副	一	亏	亏	**FUKU** (vice-, sub-, secondary)
	畐	畐	畐	副詞 *fukushi*, adverb 副会長 *fukukaichō*, vice-president (of a society) 副業 *fukugyō*, side job
709 11 strokes	畐	副	副	(刂 27)

710 復 12 strokes

FUKU (re-, again, repeat)

回復 *kaifuku*, recovery
復興 *fukkō*, revival, reconstruction [tion
復活 *fukkatsu*, revival, resurrec-
(日 11)

711 仏 4 strokes

BUTSU; *hotoke*, Buddha

大仏 *daibutsu*, colossal statue of Buddha
仏像 *butsuzō*, image of Buddha
仏教 *bukkyō*, Buddhism

712 兵 7 strokes

HEI, soldier

兵隊 *heitai*, soldier
兵器 *heiki*, arms
兵士 *heishi*, soldier

713 辺 5 strokes

HEN [PEN], side, neighborhood

底辺 *teihen*, the base (geom.)
周辺 *shūhen*, outskirts
近辺 *kimpen*, neighborhood

714 編 15 strokes

HEN; *a(mu)*, to knit, to edit

編集 *henshū*, editing
編集者 *henshūsha*, editor
編成 *hensei*, formation
(糸 83)

弁	ㄥ	ㄙ	ㄙ	**BEN**, speech
	弁	弁		弁論 *benron*, debate 弁護人 *bengonin*, counsel 弁当 *bentō*, lunch
715 5 strokes				

保	ノ	イ	亻	**HO [PO]**; *tamo(tsu)*, to keep, to maintain
	们	仴	但	保護 *hogo*, protection 保存 *hozon*, preservation 保険 *hoken*, insurance
716 9 strokes	仴	保	保	

報	土	去	去	**HŌ [PŌ]**, report; *muku(i)*, retribution; *muku(iru)*, to reward, to return (a favor)
	幸	幸	幸	報告 *hōkoku*, report 時報 *jihō*, announcement of time
717 12 strokes	幸	報	報	電報 *dempō*, telegram (土 17)

防	⁊	了	ß	**BŌ**; *fuse(gu)*, to defend, to keep off, to prevent
	ß	ß	防	予防 *yobō*, prevention 消防 *shōbō*, fire fighting
718 7 strokes	防			防波堤 *bōhatei*, breakwater

貿	ノ	ム	ム	**BŌ** (to purchase, to exchange)
	幻	切	切	貿易商 *bōekishō*, trader 貿易会社 *bōekigaisha*, trading firm
719 12 strokes	貿	貿	貿	貿易風 *bōekifū*, trade wind (目 25)

158

牧	ノ	ト	牛	BOKU ; *maki* (pasture)
	牛	牡	牪	牧場 *bokujō*, *makiba*, stock farm 牧草 *bokusō*, grass 放牧 *hōboku*, grazing
720 **8 strokes**	牧	牧		

満	氵	汁	汁	MAN, fullness; *mi(chiru)*, to fill (v. i.), to rise (tide), to wax (moon); *man~*, prefix denoting "full"
	洪	洪	満	満員 *man-in*, filled to capacity 満月 *mangetsu*, full moon 満七歳 *man-shichisai*, full seven years old
721 **12 strokes**	満	満	満	(氵 汽 60)

務	マ	予	矛	MU ; *tsuto(me)*, duties
	矛	矛	矜	事務所 *jimusho*, office 勤務 *kimmu*, service, duty 義務 *gimu*, duty
722 **11 strokes**	孜	務	務	(予 525)

無	ノ	匸	二	MU, BU ; *na(shi)* (lit.), *na(i)*, to be non-existent, not to have, to be missing, to lack, to be deceased
	仁	缶	無	無理 *muri*, unreasonable, compulsory, impossible, excessive 無線 *musen*, wireless (radio) 無事 *buji*, safe, peaceful, well
723 **12 strokes**	無	無	無	

迷	丶	丷	丷	MEI ; *mayo(u)*, to be puzzled, to lose one's way, to go astray, to be tempted by ; *mayo(wasu)*, to lead astray, to puzzle, to tempt
	半	米	米	迷信 *meishin*, superstition 迷惑 *meiwaku*, trouble, annoyance
724 **9 strokes**	米	迷	迷	

綿				MEN; *wata*, cotton
				綿屋　*wataya*, cotton shop (dealer)
				綿密　*memmitsu*, minute, careful
725 14 strokes				(糸 83,　白 37)

約				YAKU (promise, abridgment); approximately, about (prefix)
				約束　　*yakusoku*, promise, ap- pointment, regulations
				予約　　*yoyaku*, subscription, pre-engagement
726 9 strokes				約四十分　*yaku-yonjippun*, about forty minutes

輸				YU (to send)
				輸出　*yushutsu*, export
				輸血　*yuketsu*, blood transfusion
				輸送　*yusō*, transportation
727 16 strokes				(車 88)

余				YO, more (than), above; *ama(ri)*, the remainder, the balance; ~*ama- (ri)*, more than, over; *ama(ru)*, to remain, to be beyond (one's po- wer); *ama(su)*, to leave over
				余分　*yobun*, surplus
				余暇　*yoka*, spare time
728 7 strokes				余地　*yochi*, room, scope

要				YŌ, the main point, necessity; *yō(suru)*, to require, to need
				必要　*hitsuyō*, necessity, need
				要求　*yōkyū*, request, demand
729 9 strokes				重要　*jūyō*, important

容 730 10 strokes	`	‘	宀
	宀	灾	灾
	宏	宏	容

YŌ (figure; to admit)

形容詞 *keiyōshi*, adjective
内容 *naiyō*, content, substance
容積 *yōseki*, capacity, cubic measure

(口 27)

養 731 15 strokes	`	`	`
	丷	羊	羊
	美	養	養

YŌ; *yashina(u)*, to bring up, to support, to recuperate, to cultivate

教養 *kyōyō*, culture
養成 *yōsei*, training
養殖 *yōshoku*, raising, culture

(良 530)

浴 732 10 strokes	`	`	`
	``	``	``
	``	``	浴

YOKU; *a(biru)*, to bathe oneself in (water, the sun)

水浴び *mizu-abi*, bathing
入浴 *nyūyoku*, taking a bath
日光浴 *nikkō-yoku*, sun bath

(口 27)

留 733 10 strokes	`	`	厶
	幻	幻	幻
	留	留	留

RYŪ, RU; *to(meru)*, to fasten, to stop (v.t.)

停留所 *teiryūjo*, streetcar (bus) stop
留学 *ryūgaku*, studying abroad
留守 *rusu*, absence

量 734 12 strokes	`	冂	日
	日	旦	昌
	昌	量	量

RYŌ, quantity, measure; *haka(ru)*, to weigh, to measure

雨量 *uryō*, rainfall
重量 *jūryō*, weight
分量 *bunryō*, quantity

161

	令	令一	令	RYŌ (chief point; to control)
領	卻	領	領	要領 *yōryō*, the point, knack 領土 *ryōdo*, territory 領事 *ryōji*, consul
735 14 strokes	領	領	領	(令 736, 頁 169)

	ノ	人一	人	REI (proclamation, law, order)
令	令	令		号令 *gōrei*, (word of) command 命令 *meirei*, command, order 指令 *shirei*, order, instructions
736 5 strokes				

	ノ	亻	仁	REI, example
例	仃	伢	例	例外 *reigai*, exception 実例 *jitsurei*, (concrete) example 例年 *reinen*, ordinary year, every year
737 8 strokes	例	例		

	⺀	⊓	田	I; *koto*(*naru*), to be different, to be unusual
異	旦	甲	昇	異常 *ijō*, unusual 異論 *iron*, different opinion, objection ⎺nary 異様 *iyō*, strange, odd, extraordi-
738 11 strokes	畢	異	異	(田 40)

	⼝	中	虫	I, YUI (to leave behind, to bequeath)
遺	뿜	貴	貴	遺族 *izoku*, bereaved family 遺跡 *iseki*, remains, relics 遺言 *yuigon*, will, testament
739 15 strokes	遺	遺	遺	(口 27, 貝 169)

162

壱	一	十	士	ICHI, one (used in writing checks and legal documents)
	吉	声	声	壱万円　　*ichiman-en*, ten thousand yen
740 **7 strokes**	壱			壱千弐百円　*issen-nihyaku-en*, one thousand two hundred yen

営	`	``	```	EI; *itona(mi)*, occupation; *itona(mu)*, to run (a hotel), to perform (a religious service)
	𫶕	𠔼	峃	経営　*keiei*, management, operation
741 **12 strokes**	営	営		営業　*eigyō*, business, trade, operation (口 27)

益	`	``	丷	EKI, benefit, profit; *eki(suru)*, to benefit
	𠂉	关	关	利益　*rieki*, gain, benefit 有益　*yūeki*, instructive, profitable
742 **10 strokes**	益	益	益	益虫　*ekichū*, useful insect

延	ノ	亻	千	EN; *no(biru)*, to be postponed, to be extended; *no(basu)*, to postpone, to extend; *no(be)*, total
	仟	企	延	延長　*enchō*, prolongation, extension
743 **7 strokes**	延			延着　*enchaku*, late arrival 延期　*enki*, postponement

可	一	丁	𠮡	KA, good, approval
	口	可		可決　　*kaketsu*, approval 可能　　*kanō*, possibility 不可能　*fukanō*, impossibility
744 **5 strokes**				

163

我 745 7 strokes	ノ 二 千 手 我 我 我			GA; *ware*, self, oneself, I 我々 *ware-ware*, we 無我 *muga*, selflessness, ecstasy 我流 *garyū*, one's own way, self-taught method
革 746 9 strokes	一 十 廿 廿 苙 苩 苩 莒 革			KAKU (leather; to reform) 革命 *kakumei*, revolution 革新 *kakushin*, innovation, reform 改革 *kaikaku*, reform
拡 747 8 strokes	一 才 扌 扌 扩 扩 拡 拡 拡			KAKU (to extend, to unfold, to spread) 拡大 *kakudai*, magnification 拡張 *kakuchō*, extension, expansion 拡声機 *kakuseiki*, loud-speaker
額 748 18 strokes	丶 宀 宀 夕 安 客 額 額 額			GAKU, framed picture, amount (of money); *hitai*, forehead 金額 *kingaku*, amount of money 総額 *sōgaku*, sum total 多額 *tagaku*, large sum (客 184, 頁 169)
株 749 10 strokes	一 十 才 木 札 朴 杵 梯 株			*kabu*, shares, stocks, speculation in shares, stub 切り株 *kirikabu*, stump 株式会社 *kabushiki-kaisha*, joint-stock corporation 株券 *kabuken*, share certificate

164

刊 750 5 strokes	一 二 千 刊 刊	KAN (publication, edition) 刊行 *kankō*, publication 週刊 *shūkan*, weekly publication 新刊 *shinkan*, new publication
幹 751 13 strokes	一 十 吉 卓 훸 軩 軩 幹 幹	KAN; *miki*, trunk (of a tree) 幹部 *kambu*, the executive, leading members 根幹 *konkan*, basis, root 幹線 *kansen*, trunk line (早 104)
勧 752 13 strokes	ノ ト レ ケ 午 年 萑 雈 勧	KAN; *susu(meru)*, to advise, to persuade, to encourage 勧業銀行 *kangyō-ginkō*, hypothec bank 勧告 *kankoku*, advice, counsel 勧誘 *kan-yū*, invitation, canvass (力 148)
歓 753 15 strokes	レ 午 年 隹 隼 隼 歓 歓 歓	KAN (to rejoice) 歓迎 *kangei*, welcome 歓待 *kantai*, warm reception 歓談 *kandan*, pleasant talk
眼 754 11 strokes	丨 冂 目 目 目 目 眼 眼 眼	GAN; *manako*, eye 肉眼 *nikugan*, naked eye 近眼 *kingan*, near-sightedness 双眼鏡 *sōgankyō*, binoculars (目 25)

基	一	十	艹	KI; *motoi*, foundation, basis; *moto(zuku)*, to be based on
	艹	甘	其	基本 *kihon*, foundation, basis, standard
755 11 strokes	其	其	基	基地 *kichi*, (air, etc.) base 基礎 *kiso*, foundation, basis
貴	口	中	虫	KI (noble, dear, precious)
	串	毒	青	貴重 *kichō*, precious 貴金属 *kikinzoku*, precious metals 貴重品 *kichōhin*, valuables
756 12 strokes	書	貴	貴	(貝 169, 口 27)
疑	ノ	ヒ	ヒヒ	GI; *utaga(i)*, doubt, suspicion; *utaga(u)*, to doubt, to suspect
	ヒマ矢	ヒㇼ矢	ヒㇼ矛	疑問 *gimon*, question, doubt 質疑 *shitsugi*, question
757 14 strokes	ヒㇼ矛	疑	疑	疑惑 *giwaku*, suspicion, doubt (矢 112)
逆	ヽ	ヾ	丷	GYAKU, inverse, reverse; *gyaku-(ni)*, inversely, reversely; *saka(rau)*, to oppose, to go against
	屰	屰	屰	逆転 *gyakuten*, reversal, going backward
758 9 strokes	屰	逆	逆	逆境 *gyakkyō*, adversity 反逆 *hangyaku*, treason
旧	l	ll	lll	KYŪ (old)
	旧	旧		旧式 *kyūshiki*, old-style 旧跡 *kyūseki*, place of historic interest
759 5 strokes				旧暦 *kyūreki*, lunar calendar

供	ノ	イ	仁	KYŌ, GU; *tomo*, attendant; *sona-(eru)*, to offer (to a god)
	什	什	供	供給 *kyōkyū*, supply, provision 提供 *teikyō*, offer 供出 *kyōshutsu*, quota delivery
760 8 strokes	供	供		

境	土	圵	垃	KYŌ, KEI; *sakai*, border, boundary, border line
	垃	培	培	境遇 *kyōgū*, circumstances, surroundings 国境 *kokkyō*, frontier 境内 *keidai*, precincts
761 14 strokes	培	境	境	(土 17, 立 149)

勤	一	十	十十	KIN; *tsuto(me)*, duties, service; *tsuto(meru)*, to serve (in an office)
	苦	芇	革	勤務 *kimmu*, service, duty 勤勉 *kimben*, diligence 出勤 *shukkin*, attendance
762 12 strokes	菫	勤	勤	(口 27)

禁	一	十	才	KIN; *kin~*, prefix for "forbidden" or "prohibited"; *kin(jiru)*, to forbid, to abstain from
	木	林	林	禁止 *kinshi*, prohibition, ban 禁煙 *kin-en*, "No Smoking" 禁酒 *kinshu*, abstinence from alcoholic beverages
763 13 strokes	埜	禁	禁	

訓	丶	二	言	KUN (precept), Japanese rendering of a Chinese character (i.e., "kun" reading)
	言	言	言	教訓 *kyōkun*, teachings, lesson 訓練 *kunren*, training, drill 訓辞 *kunji*, address of instructions
764 10 strokes	訓	訓	訓	

				KEI (system, family line)
系	ノ	⟨	幺	系統 *keitō*, system, family line
	幺	系	系	系図 *keizu*, genealogical table
765	系	系		家系 *kakei*, family line
7 strokes				

				KEI; *uyama(u)*, to respect
敬	一	艹	艹	尊敬 *sonkei*, respect
	芍	苟	苟	敬語 *keigo*, honorific word
766	苟	敬	敬	敬意 *kei-i*, respects
12 strokes				(口 27)

				KETSU; *isagiyo(i)*, manly, brave, pure
潔	氵	氵一	氵十	清潔 *seiketsu*, clean ⌈right
	氵圭	氵圭ヲ	氵圭刀	潔白 *keppaku*, innocent, pure, up-
767	氵潔	氵潔	潔	簡潔 *kanketsu*, concise
15 strokes				(氵 汽 60, 糸 83)

				KEN, bond, ticket
券	丶	⟍	丷	定期券 *teikiken*, commutation ticket
	丷	半	关	旅券 *ryoken*, passport
768	券	券		入場券 *nyūjō-ken*, admission ticket, platform ticket
8 strokes				

				KEN, and, in addition, concurrently; *ka(neru)*, to combine, to serve in several capacities, to be unable to (suffix)
兼	丶	丷	兰	兼任 *kennin*, holding an additional post
	芈	芈	革	兼備 *kembi*, combination
769	革	兼	兼	食べ兼ねる *tabekaneru*, to be unable to eat
10 strokes				

| 險 770 11 strokes | ⁷ ⻖ 陉 陉 陰 陰 | KEN; *kewa(shii)*, steep, fierce 危険 *kiken*, danger 保険 *hoken*, insurance 冒険 *bōken*, adventure (⻖ 27) |

| 檢 771 12 strokes | 一 十 才 朩 朳 朳 朳 檢 檢 | KEN (to examine) 探検 *tanken*, exploration 検診 *kenshin*, medical examination 検定 *kentei*, official approval (⽊ 27) |

| 絹 772 13 strokes | ⼄ 乡 纟 糸 糸 紅 紅 絹 絹 | KEN; *kinu*, silk 絹糸 *kinu-ito*, silk thread 絹織物 *kinu-orimono*, silk fabrics 人絹 *jinken*, artificial silk, rayon (糸 83, ⽉ 12) |

| 憲 773 16 strokes | ⼁ ⼋ ⼧ 宀 宀 宝 實 富 憲 | KEN (law, regulation) 憲法 *kempō*, constitution 憲兵 *kempei*, military police, shore patrol 憲章 *kenshō*, charter, constitution (⼼ 95) |

| 權 774 15 strokes | 木 朮 朾 杮 枦 桥 枮 枮 權 | KEN (weight), authority, power; GON 人権 *jinken*, human rights 版権 *hanken*, copyright 政権 *seiken*, political power (⽊ 15) |

減 775 12 strokes	`丶` `氵` `氵` `氵` `沪` `沪` `沪` `減` `減` `減`	GEN; *he(ru)*, to decrease (v.i.), to wear out; *he(rasu)*, to decrease (v.t.) 加減 *kagen*, state of health, degree, adjustment, influence, addition and subtraction 減少 *genshō*, diminution, decrease 減退 *gentai*, decline, failing (口 27)

厳 776 17 strokes	`丶` `丷` `丷` `丷` `产` `产` `产` `严` `厳`	GEN, GON (severe, strict, austere) 厳禁 *genkin*, strict prohibition 厳格 *genkaku*, stern, austere 荘厳 *sōgon*, sublime, solemn (耳 26, 攵 故 778)

己 777 3 strokes	`フ` `コ` `己`	KO, KI (I, myself, oneself) 自己 *jiko*, one's self, self 利己主義 *rikoshugi*, egoism 知己 *chiki*, acquaintance, appreciative friend

故 778 9 strokes	`一` `十` `十` `古` `古` `古` `古` `故` `故`	KO (old, former times; reason) 事故 *jiko*, accident, hindrance 故郷 *kokyō*, one's native place 故障 *koshō*, mishap, trouble, accident, hindrance

誤 779 14 strokes	`丶` `二` `言` `言` `訳` `誤` `誤` `誤` `誤`	GO; *ayama(ri)*, fault, mistake, error; *ayama(ru)*, to err, to mistake 誤解 *gokai*, misunderstanding 誤字 *goji*, wrong word 誤訳 *goyaku*, mistranslation

后	´	⌐	斤	KŌ [GŌ] (empress, queen)
	斤	后	后	皇后　　*kōgō*, Empress (of Japan) 皇太后　*kōtaikō*, Empress Dowager (of Japan), Queen Mother (of England)
780 6 strokes				

孝	一	十	土	KŌ, filial duty
	耂	耂	考	孝行　*kōkō*, filial piety 孝心　*kōshin*, filial affection 孝養　*kōyō*, discharge of filial duties
781 7 strokes	孝			

効	丶	亠	亠	KŌ, efficacy, effect
	六	亥	交	効果　*kōka*, effect, efficacy, result, sound effects 効力　*kōryoku*, effect, efficacy 有効　*yūkō*, valid, effective, efficacious
782 8 strokes	効	効		

皇	´	⺊	白	KŌ, Ō (monarch, emperor)
	白	白	皇	皇太子　*kōtaishi*, Crown Prince (of Japan) 皇室　*kōshitsu*, Imperial Family (of Japan) 天皇　*tennō*, Emperor (of Japan)
783 9 strokes	皁	皁	皇	

耕	一	三	丰	KŌ; *tagaya(su)*, to till
	耒	耒	耒一	耕地　*kōchi*, arable (cultivated) land 耕作　*kōsaku*, cultivation 農耕　*nōkō*, farm labor
784 10 strokes	耒二	耕	耕	

171

構	木	村	桁	**KŌ**; *kama(e)* [*gama(e)*], structure, posture; *kama(eru)* [*gama(eru)*], to put oneself in a posture, to build
	枡	桟	樺	構成　*kōsei*, composition 構造　*kōzō*, structure, construction
785 14 strokes	構	構	構	心構え　*kokorogamae*, mental attitude, preparation

穀	士	声	声	**KOKU** (grain, cereals)
	声	壴	軎	穀物　*kokumotsu*, grain, cereals 雑穀　*zakkoku*, minor cereals 穀類　*kokurui*, cereals, grain
786 14 strokes	穀	穀	穀	(士　410,　木　15)

混	丶	氵	氵	**KON**; *ma(zeru)*, to mix, to mingle; *ma(jiru)*, to be mixed, to be mingled; *kon(zuru)*, to mix, to confound
	氵	沢	渭	混乱　*konran*, confusion 混雑　*konzatsu*, congestion, con-
787 11 strokes	泥	混	混	混合　*kongō*, mixture　└fusion

再	一	厂	冂	**SAI**, re- (prefix); *futata(bi)*, again
	丙	再	再	再建　*saiken*, reconstruction 再会　*saikai*, meeting again 再三　*saisan*, again and again
788 6 strokes				

災	く	巛	巛	**SAI**; *wazawa(i)*, disaster, misfortune
	巛	巛	災	災害　*saigai*, disaster, calamity 災難　*sainan*, misfortune, calamity 火災　*kasai*, fire, conflagration
789 7 strokes	災			

172

妻 790 8 strokes	一 ヲ ヨ / ヨ 圭 妻 / 妻 妻	SAI, my wife; *tsuma* [*zuma*], wife 夫妻　*fusai*, husband and wife 妻子　*saishi*, wife and children 妻君　*saikun*, wife
採 791 11 strokes	一 十 扌 / 扌 扩 扩 / 护 揯 採	SAI; *to(ru)*, to gather (fruit, etc.), to employ (a person), to adopt (a measure) 採集　*saishū*, collection 採用　*saiyō*, employment, adoption 採掘　*saikutsu*, mining (木 15)
済 792 11 strokes	シ ミ 汀 / 汀 汶 済 / 済 済 済	SAI [ZAI]; *su(mu)*, to end, to be settled; *su(masu)*, to finish, to pay back (a debt), to manage with (little money, etc.) 経済　*keizai*, economics, thrift 不経済　*fukeizai*, bad economy 返済　*hensai*, repayment (氵 汽 60)
財 793 10 strokes	丨 冂 月 / 目 貝 貝 / 貝一 財 財	ZAI (treasure) 財産　*zaisan*, property, fortune 財政　*zaisei*, finance(s) 私財　*shizai*, private property
罪 794 13 strokes	丶 冖 罒 / 罒 罒 罜 / 罪 罪 罪	ZAI; *tsumi*, crime, sin 犯罪　*hanzai*, crime 罪悪　*zaiaku*, sin, crime 謝罪　*shazai*, apology

策	'	⺮	⺉	SAKU, policy, scheme, measure, plan
	⺮	竺	竺	政策　*seisaku*, policy 策略　*sakuryaku*, stratagem
795 12 strokes	筞	第	策	対策　*taisaku*, counterplan

至	一	工	云	SHI [JI]; *ita(ru)*, to reach, to go so far (as to), to come, to lead to, to be brought to
	至	至	至	至急　*shikyū*, urgency 冬至　*tōji*, winter solstice
796 6 strokes				

私	'	⼆	千	SHI; *watakushi*, I, personal (affairs), privacy
	千	禾	私	私用　*shiyō*, private use (business) 私物　*shibutsu*, private property
797 7 strokes	私			私有　*shiyū*, private ownership

視	'	⼀	⼀	SHI (to look at carefully)
	⼀	礻	初	視界　*shikai*, field of vision 視力　*shiryoku*, eyesight, vision
798 11 strokes	袒	視	視	無視　*mushi*, disregard (目　25)

詞	'	⼆	言	SHI [JI] (speech, words)
	言	訂	詞	歌詞　　*kashi*, words (of a song) 名詞　　*meishi*, noun
799 12 strokes	詞			形容詞　*keiyōshi*, adjective (口　27)

174

資 800 13 strokes	`丶` `ン` `ソ` `冫` `冫` `次` `浨` `沓` `資`	SHI (wealth, help, nature) 資源 *shigen*, resources 資格 *shikaku*, capacity, qualification 物資 *busshi*, goods, materials (貝 169)
児 801 7 strokes	`丨` `刂` `冂` `旧` `旧` `旧` `児`	JI, NI (infant, child) 児童 *jidō*, child, boys and girls, juvenile 孤児 *koji*, orphan 小児まひ *shōni-mahi*, infantile paralysis
釈 802 11 strokes	`丿` `⺁` `乥` `乥` `千` `禾` `釆コ` `釈` `釈`	SHAKU (to interpret, to explain) 解釈 *kaishaku*, interpretation, explanation 会釈 *eshaku*, bow, salutation 釈放 *shakuhō*, release (米 15)
授 803 11 strokes	`一` `十` `扌` `扩` `扩` `扲` `护` `授` `授`	JU; *sazu(keru)*, to grant, to instruct; *sazu(karu)*, to be blessed with 授業 *jugyō*, lesson(s), teaching 教授 *kyōju*, teaching, professor 授賞 *jushō*, awarding a prize
需 804 14 strokes	`⺭` `币` `雨` `雫` `雫` `雫` `雫` `需` `需`	JU (to request, to demand, to await) 需要 *juyō*, demand 需給 *jukyū*, supply and demand 必需品 *hitsujuhin*, a necessity (雨 42)

宗	ヽ	´	宀
	宀	宍	宇
805 8 strokes	宇	宗	

SHŪ, SŌ (foundation, source, origin)

宗教　*shūkyō*, religion
宗派　*shūha*, sect
宗匠　*sōshō*, master (in an art), teacher

衆	宀	血	血
	血	血	衆
806 12 strokes	衆	衆	衆

SHŪ (many)

衆議院　*Shūgi-in*, House of Representatives
観衆　*kanshū*, spectators
民衆　*minshū*, the masses
(血 389)

就	亠	古	亨
	京	京	京
807 12 strokes	就	就	就

SHŪ, JU (to sit, to engage in, to be completed)

就学　*shūgaku*, entering school
就職　*shūshoku*, finding employment
成就　*jōju*, accomplishment, reali- ⌐zation
(口 27)

従	˚	彳	行
	彳	彳	彳
808 10 strokes	彳	従	従

JŪ; *shitaga(u)*, to obey, to comply with, to observe (rules), to yield to, to follow

服従　*fukujū*, obedience
従事　*jūji*, engaging in (business)
従業員　*jūgyōin*, employee

述	一	十	才
	朮	朮	术
809 8 strokes	述	述	

JUTSU; *no(beru)*, to speak, to express, to state

著述　*chojutsu*, writing (of books), one's writings
口述　*kōjutsu*, oral statement
述語　*jutsugo*, predicate (gram.)

純 810 10 strokes	く	ㄠ	幺
	纟	糸	糸
	糸	紻	純

JUN (purity, innocence)

単純　　　*tanjun*, simple
純粋　　　*junsui*, pure, genuine
純日本風　*jun-nihonfū*, purely Japanese style

| 処 811 5 strokes | ノ | ク | 夂 |
| | 処 | 処 | |

SHO; *sho(suru)*, to manage, to deal with, to sentence, to conduct oneself

処理　*shori*, management, transaction ⌐(medical)
処置　*shochi*, measure, treatment
処分　*shobun*, disposal, punishment

諸 812 15 strokes	言	訁	計
	計	訣	諸
	諸	諸	諸

SHO (many)

諸国　*shokoku*, various countries
諸君　*shokun*, gentlemen, you
諸島　*shotō*, group of islands

(言 392)

除 813 10 strokes	⁷	㇇	⻖
	⻖	阼	陉
	除	除	除

JO, division (math.); *nozo(ku)*, to take off, to remove, to exclude, to omit

除幕式　*jomakushiki*, unveiling ceremony
除名　　*jomei*, dismissal from membership
駆除　　*kujo*, extermination

招 814 8 strokes	一	十	扌
	打	扪	扪
	招	招	

SHŌ; *mane(ku)*, to invite, to beckon

招待　　*shōtai*, invitation
招待状　*shōtaijō*, invitation card

称 815 10 strokes	SHŌ (to praise); *shō(suru)*, to call, to name, to pretend 名称 *meishō*, name, denomination 略称 *ryakushō*, abbreviation 称号 *shōgō*, title
証 816 12 strokes	SHŌ (evidence, testimony) 証明 *shōmei*, proof, certification 証人 *shōnin*, witness (law), surety 保証 *hoshō*, guarantee, security (口 27)
条 817 7 strokes	JŌ (clause in a law or treaty, logic, stripe) 条件 *jōken*, terms, conditions 条約 *jōyaku*, treaty 無条件 *mujōken*, unconditional
状 818 7 strokes	JŌ (state, condition, letter) 状態 *jōtai*, state (of things), condition 現状 *genjō*, existing state of affairs, present condition 礼状 *reijō*, letter of thanks
職 819 18 strokes	SHOKU, employment, duties 職業 *shokugyō*, occupation, business 内職 *naishoku*, side job 職場 *shokuba*, place of work (耳 26, 立 149, 日 11)

仁	ノ	イ	仁	JIN, perfect virtue, benevolence, humanity
	仁			仁徳 *jintoku*, benevolence
				仁義 *jingi*, humanity and justice, humanity, duty, gamblers' moral code
820 4 strokes				仁愛 *jin-ai*, benevolence

推	一	扌	扌	SUI; *o(su)*, to infer, to guess, to recommend, to boost (a candidate)
	扩	扩	护	推理 *suiri*, reasoning
				推定 *suitei*, inference, presumption
821 11 strokes	护	推	推	推薦 *suisen*, recommendation

是	厂	口	日	ZE (right, just)
	日	旦	早	是非 *zehi*, right and wrong, by all means
				是認 *zenin*, approval
822 9 strokes	早	昃	是	是正 *zesei*, correction, revision

制	ノ	⺊	⺰	SEI (law, rule); *sei(suru)*, to restrain, to control
	乍	缶	隹	制度 *seido*, system, institution
				制服 *seifuku*, uniform
823 8 strokes	制	制		制限 *seigen*, restriction

聖	一	厂	F	SEI (sage, saint)
	王	耳	耶	聖人 *seijin*, sage, saint
				聖書 *seisho*, the Bible
				神聖 *shinsei*, sacred, holy
824 13 strokes	耶	聖	聖	(口 27)

179

誠 825 13 strokes	ニ ⇒ 言 訁 訂 訴 誠 誠 誠	SEI; *makoto*, sincerity, truth 誠実 *seijitsu*, sincerity, faithfulness 誠意 *sei-i*, sincerity, good faith 至誠 *shisei*, sincerity, one's true heart (言 392)
税 826 12 strokes	´ ⼆ 千 禾 秆 秒 秒 秒 税	ZEI, tax 税金 *zeikin*, tax 納税 *nōzei*, tax payment 税関 *zeikan*, custom house (木 15, 口 27)
舌 827 6 strokes	´ ⼆ 千 千 舌 舌	ZETSU; *shita*, tongue 舌打ち *shita-uchi*, click of the tongue, smacking one's lips 舌鼓 *shita-tsuzumi*, smacking of the lips
絶 828 12 strokes	く 幺 糸 紆 紛 絆 絡 絡 絶	ZETSU; *ta(eru)*, to cease, to become extinct 絶対 *zettai*, absoluteness 絶頂 *zetchō*, peak, zenith, summit 気絶 *kizetsu*, fainting (糸 83)
宣 829 9 strokes	` ⼆ 宀 宁 宁 宁 宣 宣 宣	SEN (to promulgate, to state) 宣言 *sengen*, declaration 宣伝 *senden*, propaganda 宣教師 *senkyōshi*, missionary

専	一 丆 丂		**SEN** (sole, exclusive)
	亐 亩 亩		専門 *semmon*, specialty
			専用 *sen-yō*, exclusive use
830 9 strokes	重 専 専		専売 *sembai*, monopoly

善	` ヽ゛ 兰		**ZEN**, good, goodness, virtue
	兰 羊 羊		親善 *shinzen*, amity, friendship
			最善 *saizen*, the best
831 12 strokes	羔 盖 善		慈善 *jizen*, charity (口 27)

創	ノ 人 ㄣ		**SŌ** (origin, beginning)
	今 合 介		創立 *sōritsu*, establishment
			創作 *sōsaku*, literary creation, original work 「tive
832 12 strokes	倉 倉 創		独創的 *dokusōteki*, original, crea- (口 27)

蔵	一 十 サ		**ZŌ**; *kura*, warehouse; *zō(suru)*, to own, to have
	芦 芦 茂		冷蔵庫 *reizōko*, refrigerator
			貯蔵 *chozō*, storage
833 15 strokes	蔵 蔵 蔵		蔵書 *zōsho*, one's library (臣 436)

俗	ノ イ 亻		**ZOKU** (customs, manners; vulgar)
	俗 俗 俗		風俗 *fūzoku*, manners, dress, popular morals
			民俗 *minzoku*, folk customs
834 9 strokes	俗 俗 俗		俗語 *zokugo*, colloquial language, slang

属	ㄱ	ㄱ	尸	**ZOKU**, genus (biol.); *zoku(suru)*, to belong to
	尸	居	犀	金属　　*kinzoku*, metal 所属　　*shozoku*, one's position 付属病院　*fuzoku-byōin*, attached hospital
835 12 strokes	属	属	属	

存	一	ナ	才	**ZON, SON** (to exist); *zon(zuru)*, to know, to think
	存	存	存	保存　*hozon*, preservation 生存　*seizon*, existence, life, survival
836 6 strokes				存在　*sonzai*, existence, being

損	一	十	扌	**SON**, loss, disadvantage; *son(suru)*, to suffer a loss
	扩	扩	捐	損害　*songai*, loss, damage 損失　*sonshitsu*, loss 破損　*hason*, damage, breakdown
837 13 strokes	捐	損	損	(口 27, 貝 169)

尊	⸝	丷	并	**SON** [ZON]; *tatto(i)*, noble, valuable; *tatto(bu)*, to respect, to value
	并	酋	酋	尊敬　*sonkei*, respect 尊重　*sonchō*, respect, deference
838 12 strokes	酋	尊	尊	本尊　*honzon*, principal image, idol

退	ㄱ	ㅋ	ヨ	**TAI**; *shirizo(ku)*, to retreat, to withdraw, to retire (v.i.); *shirizo(keru)*, to drive back, to keep away, to refuse (v.t.)
	艮	艮	艮	退場　*taijō*, leaving, walk-out, exit 退治　*taiji*, stamping out, subjugation
839 9 strokes	退	退	退	後退　*kōtai*, retreat

態	㇗	㇙	㇒	TAI [DAI] (appearance, state of affairs)
	肖	肖	肖′	態度　taido, attitude 「dition 状態　jōtai, state (of things), con- 容態　yōdai, condition (of a patient)
840 14 strokes	能	能	態	(心 95,　月 12)

断	㇔	㇔	㇓	DAN; kotowa(ru), to decline, to refuse, to give notice, to ask leave; ta(tsu), to sever, to give up (drinking), to exterminate
	米	迷	幽	断食　danjiki, a fast 油断　yudan, negligence, careless- 　　　ness, unpreparedness
841 11 strokes	断	断	断	判断　handan, judgment (米 135)

忠	丶	冂	口	CHŪ, loyalty, faithfulness
	中	中	忠	忠告　chūkoku, (friendly) advice 忠義　chūgi, loyalty 忠実　chūjitsu, faithful
842 8 strokes	忠	忠		

著	一	十	艹	CHO; ichijiru(shii), remarkable, notable, conspicuous; ara(wasu), to write (a book)
	芒	芒	芋	著書　chosho, book, work 著者　chosha, writer, author 著名　chomei, famous
843 11 strokes	芳	著	著	(目 11)

賃	ノ	イ	仁	CHIN (wages, rent)
	仁	任	任	賃金　chingin, wages 家賃　yachin, house rent 電車賃　denshachin, carfare
844 13 strokes	賃	賃	賃	(貝 169)

提	一	十	才	**TEI** (to carry in one's hand)
	扌	捍	捍	提出 *teishutsu*, presentation (of a thesis), filing (of an application)
845 12 strokes	捍	提	提	提供 *teikyō*, offer, tender (law) 提案 *teian*, suggestion, proposition

程	ノ	二	千	**TEI** (degree, rule)
	禾	和	禾口	程度 *teido*, degree, standard, limit 日程 *nittei*, day's program, schedule
846 12 strokes	禾口	程	程	行程 *kōtei*, distance (口 27, 木 15)

展	フ	コ	尸	**TEN** (to open, to exhibit)
	尸	屄	屉	展望車 *tembōsha*, observation car 発展 *hatten*, expansion, development, prosperity
847 10 strokes	屏	展	展	展示会 *tenjikai*, exhibition

党	ヽ	ン	⺌	**TŌ**, party, faction
	⺍	芯	芯	政党 *seitō*, political party 党派 *tōha*, party, faction, clique
848 10 strokes	当	労	党	

討	ヽ	二	言	**TŌ**; *u(tsu)*, to subjugate, to attack
	言	言	討	検討 *kentō*, examination, investigation
849 10 strokes	討			討論 *tōron*, debate 討議 *tōgi*, discussion

得	´	㇀	彳
	彳	犭	彳
850 11 strokes	得		

TOKU, profit, benefit, advantage; *e(ru)*, to get, to obtain
得意 *tokui*, proud satisfaction; customer; one's forte
納得 *nattoku*, understanding, compliance
得点 *tokuten*, score (in a game)
(日 11)

德	彳	彳	彳
	彳	徍	德
851 14 strokes	德	德	德

TOKU, virtue, power of commanding love and respect

道徳 *dōtoku*, morality
徳望 *tokubō*, moral influence
人徳 *jintoku*, natural virtue
(心 95, 彳 行 73)

届	㇇	㇆	尸
	尸	尸	届
852 8 strokes	届	届	

todo(ku), to reach; *todo(keru)*, to forward, to send, to report
欠席届 *kessekitodoke*, notice of one's absence
届け先 *todokesaki*, receiver's address
行き届く *yukitodoku*, to be attentive (to details), to be careful

難	一	艹	苦
	堇	革	莫
853 18 strokes	斬	斳	難

NAN, disaster, difficulty; *kata(i)*, difficult, impossible
難破 *nampa*, shipwreck
非難 *hinan*, (adverse) criticism, censure
困難 *konnan*, difficulty, trouble, ⌈suffering
(口 27, 隹 集 243)

弐	一	二	三
	三	弐	弐
854 6 strokes			

NI, two (used in legal documents)

弐千円 *nisen-en*, two thousand yen
拾弐円 *jūni-en*, twelve yen
弐百円 *nihyaku-en*, two hundred yen

認 855 14 strokes	` ` 訁 言 訒 訒 訒 訒 訒 認	NIN; *mito(meru)*, to see, to recognize; to approve of, to judge, to regard (as) 承認 *shōnin*, approval, consent, recognition 公認 *kōnin*, official recognition 認識 *ninshiki*, cognition (言 392, 心 95)
納 856 10 strokes	` ` 幺 幺 糸 糸 糸 紀 納 納	NŌ, NA, TŌ; *osa(meru)*, to put away, to pay, to supply, to dedicate, to obtain, to accept, to put back 納入 *nōnyū*, payment, delivery 納屋 *naya*, barn ⌐ments 出納 *suitō*, receipts and disburse-
派 857 9 strokes	` ` ` 氵 氵 沂 沂 沂 派	HA [PA], group, party, school 左派 *saha*, left wing, radical 派遣 *haken*, dispatch
拝 858 8 strokes	一 十 扌 扌 扌 扌 拝 拝	HAI [PAI]; *oga(mu)*, to worship, to pray to 拝見 *haiken*, inspection, looking over (polite speech) 拝啓 *haikei*, Dear Sir, Dear Madam, etc. (salutation in a let- 参拝 *sampai*, worship ⌐ter)
犯 859 5 strokes	ノ 犭 犭 犭 犯	HAN [PAN]; *oka(su)*, to commit, to violate, to rape 犯罪 *hanzai*, crime 犯人 *hannin*, criminal 防犯 *bōhan*, crime prevention

判 860 7 strokes	丶 丷 半 判	丷 半	半 判	HAN [BAN] (to decide); seal (for stamping); BAN, size 判断 *handan*, judgment, divination 裁判 *saiban*, justice, trial, judgment [book] 大判 *ō-ban*, large size (paper,
版 861 8 strokes	丿 片 版	丿 片 版	片 肟	HAN [PAN, BAN], plate, printing, edition 版画 *hanga*, woodblock print 版権 *hanken*, copyright 出版 *shuppan*, publication
否 862 7 strokes	一 不 否	丆 不	不 否	HI [PI]; *ina*, no 否定 *hitei*, denial 拒否 *kyohi*, refusal, rejection 安否 *ampi*, safety, well-being
評 863 12 strokes	丶 言 訂	二 訂 証	言 訂 評	HYŌ [PYŌ], criticism; *hyō(suru)*, to criticize, to comment 評判 *hyōban*, reputation, popularity, rumor 評価 *hyōka*, appraisal, appreciation 批評 *hihyō*, criticism [tion] (言 392)
富 864 12 strokes	丶 宫 富	丶 宫 富	宀 宫 富	FU [PU], (FŪ); *tomi*, riches; *to(mu)*, to be rich, to abound (in) 豊富 *hōfu*, abundance 富貴 *fuki, fūki, fukki*, rich and noble 富裕 *fuyū*, riches, wealth (宀 27)

複	ラ ネ ネ		FUKU (to repeat); prefix for "double"	
	ネ ネ ネ		複雑 *fukuzatsu*, complication, complexity	
865 14 strokes	複 複 複		複製 *fukusei*, reproduction 重複 *chōfuku*, *jūfuku*, duplication, repetition	

奮	大 太 本		FUN; *furu(u)*, to rouse oneself	
	本 本 奔		興奮 *kōfun*, excitement 奮闘 *funtō*, hard fighting, strenuous efforts	
866 16 strokes	奮 奮 奮		発奮 *happun*, being inspired, rousing oneself (大 22, 田 40)	

陛	了 阝 阝		HEI (stairs of a palace)	
	阝 阝ノ 阝比		陛下 *heika*, His (Her) Majesty, Your Majesty 天皇陛下 *tennō-heika*, His Majesty the Emperor (of Japan)	
867 10 strokes	陛 陛 陛		皇后陛下 *kōgō-heika*, Her Majesty the Empress (of Japan)	

補	ラ ネ ネ		HO; *ogina(u)*, to supply, to compensate (for), to supplement	
	补 衤 袻		候補 *kōho*, candidacy, candidate 補助 *hojo*, assistance, supplement, subsidy	
868 12 strokes	袻 補 補		補給 *hokyū*, supply	

墓	一 十 艹		BO; *haka*, grave	
	苩 苩 莫		墓地 *bochi*, graveyard 墓石 *boseki*, *haka-ishi*, gravestone	
869 13 strokes	莫 莫 墓		墓参 *bosan*, visit to a grave (日 早 104, 土 17)	

188

豊	冂	曲	曲	HŌ; *yuta(ka)*, abundance
				豊年　*hōnen*, year of abundance
	曲	曲	曹	豊作　*hōsaku*, good harvest
870 13 strokes	曹	豊	豊	(曲 381, 冂 27)

暴	日	旦	昇	BŌ, BAKU (violent; to disclose)
				暴力　*bōryoku*, violence, force
	显	昇	異	乱暴　*rambō*, violence, unreason- ableness
871 15 strokes	暴	暴	暴	暴露　*bakuro*, disclosure (日 旱 104)

未	一	二	丰	MI (yet, never, till now, un-)
				未来　*mirai*, future
	才	未		未開　*mikai*, uncivilized, unculti- vated
872 5 strokes				未知　*michi*, unknown, strange

盟	冂	日	明	MEI (to swear, to pledge)
				連盟　*remmei*, league
	明	明	盟	同盟　*dōmei*, alliance
				加盟　*kamei*, joining (an alliance), participation
873 13 strokes	盟	盟	盟	(明 141)

訳	二	言	言	YAKU, translation; *wake*, reason, meaning, circumstances; *yaku(su- ru)*, to translate
	訂	訂	訳	翻訳　　*hon-yaku*, translation 通訳　　*tsūyaku*, interpretation, in- terpreter
874 11 strokes	訳			言い訳　*iiwake*, excuse, apology (言 392)

189

預 875 13 strokes	フ マ ヲ 予 予 予 預 預 預	YO; *azu(karu)*, to keep, to take charge of, to refrain from, to receive; *azu(keru)*, to deposit, to put into the charge of 預金 *yokin*, money on deposit 預り物 *azukarimono*, item left in someone's charge 預り証 *azukarishō*, deposit receipt (阝 169)
欲 876 11 strokes	' ハ ハ 父 谷 谷 欲 欲 欲	YOKU, avarice, desire; *hos(suru)*, to desire, to wish 欲ばり *yokubari*, greedy person, miser 欲望 *yokubō*, desire 食欲 *shokuyoku*, appetite (口 27)
律 877 9 strokes	' ク イ 行 行 行 律 律 律	RITSU (law, degree) 法律 *hōritsu*, law 規律 *kiritsu*, order, discipline, regulations 旋律 *senritsu*, melody
率 878 11 strokes	' 亠 玄 玄 玄 玄 率 率 率	RITSU, rate; SOTSU; *hiki(iru)*, to lead, to command 能率 *nōritsu*, efficiency 出席率 *shussekiritsu*, percentage of attendance 統率 *tōsotsu*, command, leadership (玄 糸 83)
略 879 11 strokes	' 冂 冊 冊 田 田 田' 田ノ 略 略	RYAKU, abbreviation, omission, outline; *ryaku(suru)*, to omit 計略 *keiryaku*, stratagem, plan, plot 省略 *shōryaku*, omission 略称 *ryakushō*, abbreviation (口 27)

臨	⼁	厂	卩	RIN; *nozo(mu)*, to face, to meet, to be present at
	臣	臣'	臣⼂	臨終 *rinjū*, the hour of death 臨時 *rinji*, special, extra, tempo- 臨席 *rinseki*, attendance ⌐rary
880 18 strokes	臨	臨	臨	(口 27, 臣 436)
論	言	訃	論	RON, argument, opinion, essay
	論	論	論	結論 *ketsuron*, conclusion 討論 *tōron*, debate, discussion 理論 *riron*, theory
881 15 strokes	論	論	論	(言 392)

191

The 1,850
GENERAL-USE CHARACTERS

1 STROKE

一	1 page 15	乙	OTSU, 2nd in a series, .grade B; chic, witty; strange

2 STROKES

丁	473 page 109	入	125 page 40
七	7 page 16	八	8 page 16
九	9 page 16	刀	289 page 72
了	RYŌ (to come to an end, to understand)	力	148 page 44
二	2 page 15	十	10 page 17
人	30 page 21	又	*mata*, and, again, also

3 STROKES

丈	JŌ, old unit of length (3.316 yd.), length	千	101 page 35
三	3 page 15	及	KYŪ; oyo(bi), and; oyo(bu), to reach, to equal, to extend
上	20 page 19	口	27 page 20
下	21 page 19	土	17 page 18
丸	GAN, suffix denoting a pill; maru(i), round, circular, globular	士	410 page 97
久	582 page 131	夕	98 page 34
亡	BŌ (to lose, to perish, to be non-existent, to flee); the late (prefix for " deceased ")	大	22 page 19
凡	BON (generally, all, roughly, ordinary)	女	32 page 21
刃	JIN; ha, edge (of a knife, sword, etc.), blade	子	31 page 21
勺	SHAKU, old unit of capacity (0.152 gi.), old unit of area (0.355 sq.ft.)	寸	SUN, old unit of length (1.193 in.), measure

小	24 page 19	干	KAN; ho(su), to dry, to air, to drain off (v.t.); hi(ru), to dry (v.i.), to ebb
山	38 page 22	弓	KYŪ; *yumi*, bow, archery
川	39 page 22	才	217 page 58
工	71 page 29	与	YO; ata(eru), to give, to award, to supply, to cause (damage), to assign (a task)
己	777 page 170	万	320 page 79

4 STROKES

不	500 page 115	五	5 page 16
中	23 page 19	井	SEI, SHŌ; *i* (lit.), well (n.)
丹	TAN (cinnabar, red; elixir of life)	仁	820 page 179
乏	BŌ; tobo(shii), scanty, short (of food, money)	今	81 page 31
互	GO; taga(i), each other, one another, mutual	介	KAI (to come between, to aid); kai-(shite), through the good offices of

仏	711 page 157	化	163 page 47
元	68 page 28	匹	HITSU (an equal); HIKI, suffix for counting small ani- mals, rolls of cloth
内	489 page 112	区	591 page 133
公	210 page 57	升	SHŌ, old unit of ca- pacity (3.81 pt.)
六	6 page 16	午	207 page 56
冗	JŌ (waste, useless- ness, surplus)	友	145 page 44
凶	KYŌ (evil, calamity)	反	492 page 113
分	133 page 41	円	48 page 24
切	99 page 34	天	119 page 38
刈	ka(ru), to mow, to reap, to prune, to shear, to cut (hair)	太	269 page 68
匁	momme, old unit of weight (2.117 dr.)	夫	501 page 115

孔	KŌ (hole; extremely; to pass)	文	134 page 41
少	93 page 33	斗	TO, old unit of capacity (19.04 qt.), one-*to* measure
尺	SHAKU, old measure of length (0.995 ft.), length	斤	KIN, old unit of weight (1.323 lb.)
幻	GEN; *maboroshi*, vision, phantom	方	138 page 42
弔	CHŌ; *tomura(i)*, funeral, condolence; *tomura(u)*, to condole, to mourn	日	11 page 17
引	156 page 46	月	12 page 17
心	95 page 34	木	15 page 18
戸	69 page 28	止	220 page 59
手	28 page 20	比	697 page 154
支	621 page 139	毛	142 page 43
収	631 page 141	氏	620 page 139

水	14 page 17	犬	66 page 28
火	13 page 17	王	49 page 24
父	131 page 41	欠	597 page 134
片	HEN, scrap, piece; *kata* (one of a pair, one side, the other one)	予	525 page 120
牛	62 page 27	双	SŌ (both, pair; to rival)

5 STROKES

且	*ka(tsu)*, besides, moreover, at the same time	仕	221 page 59
世	263 page 67	他	459 page 106
丘	KYŪ; *oka*, hill	付	502 page 115
丙	HEI, 3rd class, the 3rd in a series, grade C	代	463 page 107
主	237 page 62	令	736 page 162

以	342 page 83	占	SEN; *urana(i)*, divination; *urana(u)*, to divine; *shi(meru)*, to occupy, to hold (a seat)
兄	199 page 54	去	189 page 52
冊	SATSU, suffix for counting books and magazines	古	70 page 29
冬	120 page 39	句	592 page 133
出	90 page 33	召	SHŌ; *me(su)*, honorific for "to wear," "to summon"
刊	750 page 165	可	744 page 163
功	605 page 136	史	411 page 97
加	356 page 86	右	19 page 18
包	511 page 117	司	412 page 97
北	139 page 42	囚	SHŪ (to capture; captivity, slavery, prisoner)
半	129 page 40	四	4 page 15

圧	544 page 123	布	706 page 156
外	56 page 26	平	315 page 78
央	554 page 125	幼	YŌ; *osana(i)*, infant, childish
失	418 page 98	広	211 page 57
奴	DO (manservant, fellow, guy)	庁	CHŌ (government office, board)
写	419 page 98	必	497 page 114
尼	NI; *ama*, nun	打	460 page 107
左	18 page 18	払	FUTSU; *hara(u)*, to pay, to clear away, to lop off (branches), to dispose of
巧	KŌ; *taku(mi)*, skill	斥	SEKI (to drive away, to keep away, to refuse)
巨	KYO (many, much, huge, gigantic)	未	872 page 189
市	222 page 59	末	515 page 118

199

本	45 page 24	生	34 page 21
札	SATSU, bill, paper money; *fuda*, card, label, tag, ticket, charm	用	146 page 44
正	46 page 24	田	40 page 23
母	137 page 42	由	325 page 80
民	518 page 118	甲	KŌ, grade A, the former; back (of the hand); shell (of a tortoise); KAN
氷	498 page 114	申	254 page 65
永	550 page 125	白	37 page 22
犯	859 page 186	皮	307 page 76
玄	GEN (dark, black, abstruse; heaven; quiet)	目	25 page 20
玉	64 page 27	矛	MU (halberd)
甘	KAN; *ama(i)*, sweet, indulgent, flattering, over-optimistic, easy to deal with	矢	*ya*, arrow

石	44 page 23	旧	759 page 166
示	622 page 139	処	811 page 177
礼	337 page 82	号	215 page 58
穴	KETSU; *ana*, hole, burrow, cave; deficit; unexpected win	弁	715 page 158
立	149 page 44	込	*ko(mu)*, to be crowded; *ko(meru)*, to load (a gun), to include; to concentrate (on)
台	272 page 69	辺	713 page 157

6 STROKES

交	212 page 57	任	688 page 152
仰	GYŌ, KŌ; *ao(gu)*, to look up at (to), to ask for; *ō(se)*, another's word or instructions	企	KI; *kuwada(te)*, attempt, plan, intrigue; *kuwada(teru)*, to attempt, to plan
仲	CHŪ; *naka*, relations (between persons), terms	伏	FUKU; *fu(seru)*, to turn over (v.t.), to cover, to conceal, to lay (an ambush)
件	598 page 134	伐	BATSU (to attack, to fell; to boast)

休	61 page 27	刑	KEI, punishment, penalty
仮	559 page 126	列	537 page 122
伝	681 page 151	劣	RETSU; oto(ru), to be inferior
充	JŪ (to fill); a(teru), to allot, to appropriate	匠	SHŌ (carpenter, artisan)
兆	CHŌ, trillion (U.S.), billion (Eng.); sign, symptom, portent	印	348 page 84
先	33 page 21	危	KI; ayau(i), dangerous, unsafe, doubtful, unsteady
光	72 page 29	叫	KYŌ; sake(bu), to exclaim, to shout, to cry for
全	267 page 68	各	568 page 128
両	336 page 82	合	77 page 30
共	376 page 90	吉	KICHI, good luck, good omen
再	788 page 172	同	295 page 74

名	140 page 43	壮	SŌ (powerful, influential, brave)
后	780 page 171	多	108 page 36
吏	RI (an official)	好	KŌ; kono(mu), su(ku), to like, to love, to take delight in
吐	TO; ha(ku), to vomit, to spew, to emit, to confess, to express	如	JO, NYO (as if, looking like; to equal, to reach)
向	213 page 57	妃	HI (empress, married princess)
吸	KYŪ; su(u), to sip, to breathe in, to suck, to absorb, to smoke (tobacco)	字	86 page 32
回	168 page 48	存	836 page 182
因	548 page 124	宅	TAKU, home, our home, my husband
団	672 page 149	宇	U (eaves, house, sky)
在	613 page 137	守	421 page 99
地	111 page 37	安	153 page 45

寺	228 page 60	旬	JUN (period of ten days)
州	424 page 99	曲	381 page 91
巡	JUN; *megu(ru)*, to go one's rounds, to patrol, to travel about	会	54 page 25
帆	HAN; *ho*, sail, canvas	有	523 page 119
年	126 page 40	朱	SHU, cinnabar, vermilion
式	417 page 98	机	KI; *tsukue*, desk
忙	BŌ; *isoga(shii)*, busy	朽	KYŪ; *ku(chiru)*, to rot, to perish, to remain in obscurity
成	439 page 102	次	227 page 60
扱	*atsuka(u)*, to deal with, to receive, to manage, to deal in, to work (manipulate)	死	223 page 59
旨	SHI; *mune*, purport, effect, principle, command	毎	318 page 78
早	104 page 35	気	59 page 26

汗	KAN; *ase*, sweat	糸	83 page 31
汚	O; *kega(su)*, to bring disgrace upon, to soil; *kega(reru)*, to be dishonored, to get dirty	羊	YŌ; *hitsuji*, sheep, lamb, ewe, ram
江	KŌ; *e* (inlet, bay)	羽	U; *ha*, *hane*, wing, feather
池	110 page 37	老	541 page 123
灰	KAI; *hai*, ashes	考	74 page 29
争	451 page 105	耳	26 page 20
当	290 page 73	肉	297 page 74
百	130 page 41	自	229 page 60
尽	JIN; *tsu(kusu)*, to render service to; to exhaust, to use up	至	796 page 174
竹	113 page 37	舌	827 page 180
米	135 page 42	舟	SHŪ; *fune*, boat, ship

色	94 page 33	行	73 page 29
芋	*imo*, taro, Irish potato, sweet potato, etc.	衣	341 page 83
芝	*shiba*, turf, grass	西	96 page 34
虫	114 page 37	弐	854 page 185
血	389 page 92	迅	JIN (swift, quick, fast)

7 STROKES

乱	RAN, civil war, riot; *mida(reru)*, to be disordered; *mida(su)*, to throw into disorder	伺	SHI; *ukaga(u)*, to visit, to ask, to hear
亜	A, sub~, near~ (used as prefix)	似	625 page 140
伯	HAKU (a count, a chief, elder brother)	但	*tada(shi)*, but, provided (that)
伴	HAN, BAN; *tomo(nau)*, to accompany, to take with	位	344 page 83
伸	SHIN; *no(biru)*, to extend, to grow; to collapse (v.i.); *no(basu)*, to lengthen, to stretch	低	677 page 150

住	244 page 63	判	860 page 187
佐	SA (to help)	別	508 page 116
何	51 page 25	利	528 page 120
作	82 page 31	助	248 page 64
体	270 page 69	努	481 page 111
来	147 page 44	労	542 page 123
克	KOKU (to be able to do, to conquer)	励	REI; *hage(mu)*, to strive, to make an effort
児	801 page 175	却	KYAKU (to reject, to withdraw)
兵	712 page 157	卵	RAN; *tamago*, egg, spawn, hen's egg; (in) embryo
冷	535 page 122	即	SOKU (at once; namely, nothing but; accession)
初	428 page 100	君	198 page 54

吟	GIN; gin(zuru), to recite (a poem)	均	590 page 133
否	862 page 187	坊	BŌ, sonny, boy, priest, priest's lodge
含	GAN; fuku(mu), to contain, to include, to keep in one's mouth, to harbor, to cherish	坑	KŌ (hole, mine pit, cave)
呈	TEI; tei(suru), to offer (congratulations), to present (a tragic sight)	壱	740 page 163
呉	GO (ancient province of China)	寿	JU; kotobuki, congratulations; longevity
吹	SUI; fu(ku), to blow, to breathe out, to play (a wind instrument), to talk big	妊	NIN (to conceive, to become pregnant)
告	398 page 94	妙	MYŌ, strange, mysterious; clever, admirable
困	KON; koma(ru), to be troubled, to be perplexed, to be badly off	妥	DA (peaceful, calm)
囲	343 page 83	妨	BŌ; samata(geru), to obstruct, to disturb, to prevent
図	261 page 67	孝	781 page 171
坂	304 page 75	完	571 page 129

対	461 page 107	形	200 page 55
尾	BI, suffix for counting fish; *o*, tail, ridge, trail (of a shooting star)	役	324 page 79
尿	NYŌ, urine	忌	KI; *i(mu)*, to abhor, to detest, to avoid, to taboo
局	194 page 53	忍	NIN; *shino(bu)*, to bear (pain), to endure; to conceal oneself
岐	KI (fork of a road)	志	623 page 139
希	575 page 130	忘	BŌ; *wasu(reru)*, to forget, to fail to notice, to leave behind
床	SHŌ; *toko*, bed, alcove; *yuka*, floor	快	566 page 128
序	638 page 142	応	556 page 126
延	743 page 163	我	745 page 164
廷	TEI (public office)	戒	KAI; *imashi(meru)*, to admonish, to warn; *imashi(me)*, admonition, warning, lesson
弟	282 page 71	扶	FU (to help)

批	HI (to criticize; to strike)	更	KŌ (to change, to renew, to reform); *sara-(ni)*, anew, again, still more, (not) at all
技	579 page 130	材	403 page 95
抄	SHŌ (to excerpt; extract, excerpt)	村	107 page 36
抑	YOKU (to restrain, to hold down, to stop)	束	SOKU, suffix for counting bundles; *ta-ba*, bundle, bunch
投	291 page 73	条	817 page 178
抗	KŌ (to resist, to confront)	求	583 page 131
折	651 page 145	決	202 page 55
抜	BATSU; *nu(ku)*, to pull out, to outstrip, to omit, to remove, to capture	汽	60 page 27
択	TAKU (to choose, to select, to sort out)	沈	CHIN; *shizu(mu)*, to sink, to feel depressed
改	359 page 86	没	BOTSU, rejection (of a manuscript); *bos-(suru)*, to sink, to set (sun), to die
攻	KŌ; *se(meru)*, to attack, to assault; *se-(me)*, attack	沖	*oki*, offing, open sea

沢	TAKU ; *sawa*, marsh, swamp	声	97 page 34
災	789 page 172	肖	SHŌ (to resemble, to pattern after, to copy after)
状	818 page 178	肝	KAN (vital point) ; *kimo*, the liver ; pluck, mind
狂	KYŌ, ~addict ; *kuru-(i)*, disorder, warp ; *kuru(u)*, to go mad, to get out of order	臣	436 page 102
男	109 page 36	良	530 page 121
町	115 page 38	花	43 page 23
社	234 page 61	芳	HŌ ; *kamba(shii)*, fragrant
秀	SHŪ, excellent ; (to surpass, to excel)	芽	358 page 86
私	797 page 174	芸	388 page 92
究	185 page 52	見	67 page 28
系	765 page 168	角	173 page 49

言	392 page 93	迎	GEI; *muka(eru)*, to meet, to welcome, to invite; *muka(e)*, meeting, greeter
谷	78 page 30	近	195 page 54
豆	TŌ, ZU; *mame*, peas, beans; *mame~*, baby ~, midget~ (prefix for "miniature")	返	316 page 78
貝	169 page 48	邦	HŌ (country, land)
売	301 page 75	邪	JA, wrong, injustice, evil
赤	35 page 22	医	345 page 84
走	105 page 36	里	332 page 81
足	29 page 20	防	718 page 158
身	255 page 66	余	728 page 160
車	88 page 32	麦	128 page 40
辛	SHIN (bitter, hard, severe); *kara(i)*, pungent, spicy, hot, salty		

8 STROKES

乳	NYŪ; *chichi*, *chi*, milk, breasts	侮	BU; *anado(ru)*, to look down upon, to hold in contempt
事	230 page 61	併	HEI (to amalgamate, to combine)
亨	KYŌ (to receive, to enjoy)	価	563 page 127
京	63 page 27	免	MEN; *manuka(reru)*, to escape, to avoid, to be exempt; *men(zuru)*, to dismiss, to excuse
佳	KA, good, beautiful	具	383 page 91
使	224 page 59	典	680 page 151
例	737 page 162	到	TŌ (to reach, to go or come to)
侍	JI (samurai); *ji(suru)*, to attend on	制	823 page 179
供	760 page 167	刷	405 page 96
依	I, E (to depend on)	券	768 page 168

213

刺	SHI (name card; thorn, splinter); sa-(su), to sting, to pierce, to stab	受	240 page 63
刻	KOKU; kiza(mu), to cut fine, to hash, to chop, to carve (an image)	周	632 page 141
効	782 page 171	味	516 page 118
劾	GAI (to investigate thoroughly)	呼	KO; yo(bu), to call, to send for, to invite, to attract, to bring about, to name
卒	457 page 106	命	519 page 118
卓	TAKU (to excel, to surpass); table, desk	和	338 page 82
協	377 page 90	固	393 page 93
卸	oro(su), to sell wholesale; oroshi, wholesale	国	79 page 30
参	616 page 138	坪	tsubo, old unit of area (3.952 sq. yd.)
叔	SHUKU (younger brother of one's parent)	垂	SUI (to hang, to dangle, to droop)
取	238 page 62	夜	144 page 43

· 214 ·

奇	KI (unusual, rare, surpassing, strange, mysterious)	宗	805 page 176
奉	HŌ; *tatematsu(ru)*, to offer, to revere; *hō-(zuru)*, to believe in, to present, to obey	官	364 page 87
奔	HON (to run)	宙	CHŪ (heaven, sky, space)
妹	319 page 78	定	474 page 109
妻	790 page 173	宜	GI (all right, good, just, proper, natural)
姉	413 page 97	実	233 page 61
始	225 page 60	宝	HŌ; *takara*, treasure, riches
姓	SEI, surname, family name; SHŌ	居	586 page 132
委	346 page 84	届	852 page 185
季	369 page 88	屈	KUTSU; *kus(suru)*, to yield to, to be daunted, to bend
学	57 page 26	岩	178 page 50

岸	177 page 50	忠	842 page 183
岳	GAKU; *take* (lit.), peak, mountain	念	689 page 152
幸	395 page 94	怖	FU (to fear, to be afraid)
底	475 page 110	性	645 page 144
店	284 page 71	怪	KAI, mystery, apparition; *aya(shii)*, suspicious; *aya(shimu)*, to doubt, to suspect
府	503 page 115	房	BŌ (chamber, house; bunch, cluster, tuft)
弦	GEN, *tsuru*, string (for musical instruments), bowstring, chord	所	246 page 64
彼	HI; *kare*, he; *ka(no)*, that	承	639 page 142
往	555 page 126	抱	HŌ; *da(ku)*, to hold in one's arms, to hug, to sit (on eggs)
征	SEI (to subjugate)	抵	TEI (to touch, to go against)
径	KEI (path, lane, method; diameter; immediately)	押	Ō; *o(su)*, to push, to press; *o(shi)*, influence, audacity; *osa(eru)*, to repress

抽	CHŪ (to draw out, to pull)	放	512 page 117
拍	HAKU, HYŌ (to clap; musical time, beat)	昇	SHŌ (to rise, to go up)
拒	KYO; *koba(mu)*, to refuse, to decline, to resist, to deny	明	141 page 43
拓	TAKU (clearing, reclamation; production of copies by rubbing)	易	545 page 124
拘	KŌ (to catch, to affect, to adhere to)	昔	SEKI, SHAKU; *mukashi*, ancient times, bygone days; long ago, formerly
拙	SETSU (clumsy, unskillful, inexpert)	服	505 page 116
招	814 page 177	杯	HAI, suffix for counting cupfuls, glassfuls, etc.; *sakazuki*, saké cup
拝	858 page 186	東	121 page 39
担	TAN (to carry on the shoulder; to deceive; to be superstitious)	松	SHŌ; *matsu*, pine, pine tree
拠	KYO, KO (to depend on, to be based on, to hold; foundation, ground, authority)	板	305 page 76
拡	747 page 164	析	SEKI (to divide, to tear, to break)

林	150 page 45	沸	FUTSU; *wa(ku)*, to boil, to seethe, to ferment (v.i.)
枚	MAI, suffix for counting thin or flat things	油	522 page 119
果	560 page 127	治	468 page 108
枝	SHI; *eda*, branch, bough, twig	沼	SHŌ; *numa*, swamp, marsh, bog
枢	SŪ (pivot, vital point, center)	沿	EN; *so(u)*, to go (be) along, to be on (beside)
欧	Ō (Europe)	況	KYŌ (state of things; still more)
殴	Ō (to beat, to strike)	泊	HAKU; *to(maru)*, to stay overnight, to stop over; *to(meru)*, to lodge (v.t.)
歩	136 page 42	泌	HITSU (to ooze out)
武	708 page 156	法	513 page 117
毒	686 page 152	波	298 page 74
河	561 page 127	泣	KYŪ; *na(ku)*, to cry, to weep, to blubber

注	277 page 70	直	472 page 109
泳	352 page 85	知	112 page 37
炊	SUI (to cook, to boil)	祈	KI; *ino(ru)*, to pray, to invoke, to wish; *ino(ri)*, prayer, wish
炎	EN (to burn); *hono-o*, flame, blaze	祉	SHI (blessing, happiness)
炉	**RO, fireplace, hearth, smelting furnace**	空	65 page 28
版	861 page 187	突	TOTSU (sudden); *tsu(ku)*, to pierce, to thrust, to strike, to attack
牧	720 page 159	並	HEI; *nami*, ordinary; *nara(beru)*, to place in order; *nara(bu)*, to line up; *nara(bini)*, and
物	313 page 77	者	235 page 62
画	167 page 48	肥	699 page 154
的	478 page 110	肩	KEN; *kata*, shoulder
盲	MŌ; *mekura*, blindness, blind person; ignorance	肪	BŌ (fat, grease, tallow)

肯	KŌ (to consent, to agree; daringly, boldly)	迭	TETSU (to change places with; by turns)
育	347 page 84	述	809 page 176
舎	629 page 140	邸	TEI (mansion, residence)
苗	BYŌ; *nae*, seedling, sapling	金	16 page 18
若	JAKU; *waka(i)*, young, younger, immature, low (number); *mo(shikuwa)*, or	長	116 page 38
苦	197 page 54	門	143 page 43
英	353 page 85	阻	SO (steep; to separate, to obstruct)
茂	MO; *shige(ru)*, to grow thick, to grow rank	附	FU (to stick to, to adhere to)
茎	KEI; *kuki*, stalk, stem	雨	42 page 23
表	309 page 76	青	36 page 22
迫	HAKU; *sema(ru)*, to press, to urge, to draw near	非	698 page 154

9 STROKES

乗	251 page 65	冒	BŌ; *oka(su)*, to brave, to defy, to attack, to damage, to profane
侯	KŌ (feudal lord; marquis)	冠	KAN; *kammuri*, crown
侵	SHIN; *oka(su)*, to invade, to violate	則	666 page 148
係	385 page 92	削	SAKU; *kezu(ru)*, to shave (wood), to sharpen, to delete, to curtail
便	510 page 117	前	102 page 35
促	SOKU; *unaga(su)*, to urge	勅	CHOKU (Imperial edict)
俊	SHUN (to be excellent, to surpass, to be high)	勇	524 page 119
俗	834 page 181	卑	HI; *iya(shii)*, base, vulgar, low-lived; *iya(shimeru)*, to despise
保	716 page 158	南	124 page 39
信	437 page 102	巻	KAN, volume, reel (used as suffix); *maki*, volume, roll; *ma(ku)*, to roll, to wind (v.t.)

厘	RIN, old unit of money (0.001 yen); old unit of length (about 0.0119 in.)	姿	SHI; *sugata*, figure, shape, appearance, aspect, condition
厚	606 page 136	威	I (majestic, solemn; to threaten)
咲	*sa(ku)*, to bloom, to blossom	孤	KO (orphan; solitary, alone)
哀	AI; *awa(re)*, pathos, misery, pity; *awa(re-mu)*, to feel pity for	客	184 page 51
品	311 page 77	宣	829 page 180
単	671 page 149	室	232 page 61
型	595 page 134	封	FŪ, seal; *fū(zuru)*, to prevent, to enclose, to blockade, to seal; HŌ, fief
城	JŌ; *shiro*, castle	専	830 page 181
奏	SŌ; *sō(suru)*, to play (music, a musical instrument); to report to the Throne	屋	161 page 47
契	KEI; *chigi(ru)*, to pledge, to promise	峠	*tōge*, mountain pass, ridge, peak, crisis
姻	IN (to get married)	峡	KYŌ (gorge, ravine)

222

帝	TEI (emperor, sovereign, Mikado)	怠	TAI; okota(ru), to neglect, to be idle
帥	SUI (to command an army)	急	186 page 52
幽	YŪ (faint, profound, quiet)	恒	KŌ (always, eternal)
度	288 page 72	恨	KON; ura(mi), spite, grudge; ura(mu), to bear a grudge against, to regret
建	391 page 93	悔	KAI; ku(iru), to regret; kuya(mi), condolence; kuya(mu), to mourn, to repent
弧	KO, arc	括	KATSU (to fasten, to bind, to tie up)
待	271 page 69	拷	GŌ (to beat, to strike)
律	877 page 190	拾	425 page 100
後	208 page 56	持	231 page 61
怒	DO; ika(ru) (lit.), to get angry	指	226 page 60
思	84 page 31	政	646 page 144

故	778 page 170	架	KA; ka(suru), to build, to span (a river with a bridge, etc.)
叙	JO (preface); jo(su-ru), to describe; to confer (a rank) upon	柄	HEI; e, handle; gara, pattern, design, build, character, nature
施	SHI, SE; hodoko(su), to give in charity; to perform, to administer	某	BŌ, a certain person, Mr. So-and-so; one, a, a certain~ (used as prefix)
星	264 page 67	染	SEN; so(meru), to dye; so(maru), to be dyed, to be imbued
映	EI; utsu(ru), to be reflected, to match (v.i.); utsu(su), to project on a screen, to reflect	柔	JŪ, NYŪ; yawa(ra-kai), soft, tender, mild, mellow
春	91 page 33	査	611 page 137
昨	404 page 95	柱	278 page 70
昭	249 page 64	柳	RYŪ; yanagi, willow tree
是	822 page 179	栄	549 page 124
昼	279 page 70	段	DAN, degree, step, grade, platform
枯	KO; ka(reru), to wither, to mature (v.i.); ka(rasu), to blight	泉	SEN; izumi, spring, fountain

洋	526 page 120	狩	SHU; *ka(ri)*, hunting, gathering, (maple-, etc.) viewing; *ka(ru)*, to hunt
洗	SEN; *ara(u)*, to wash; to inquire into (a person's past)	狭	KYŌ; *sema(i)*, narrow, small
津	*tsu*, harbor, ferry	独	687 page 152
活	174 page 49	珍	CHIN; *mezura(shii)*, rare, novel, unusual
派	857 page 186	界	170 page 49
海	55 page 26	畑	302 page 75
浄	JŌ (pure, innocent)	疫	EKI (epidemic)
浅	655 page 146	発	303 page 75
炭	274 page 69	皆	KAI; *mina*, all, everything, everyone
為	I (to do, to make, to think; benefit, reason, cause, purpose)	皇	783 page 171
牲	SEI (sacrifice, victim)	盆	BON, tray; the Bon festival (Buddhist celebration held in Japan in mid-July)

県	203 page 55	秋	89 page 32
相	452 page 105	科	164 page 47
盾	JUN (shield)	秒	499 page 114
省	640 page 143	窃	SETSU (to steal, to rob)
看	KAN (to watch, to pay a visit of inquiry, to see from afar)	糾	KYŪ (to investigate, to examine; to twist, to twine around)
砂	SHA, SA; *suna*, sand	紀	578 page 130
研	204 page 55	約	726 page 160
砕	SAI; *kuda(ku)*, to break into pieces, to smash; to explain in simple words	紅	KŌ, KU; *kurenai*, crimson; *beni*, rouge, lipstick; crimson
祖	657 page 146	級	187 page 52
祝	635 page 142	美	308 page 76
神	257 page 66	耐	TAI; *ta(eru)*, to endure, to bear, to stand (v.t.)

肺	HAI, lung	虐	GYAKU (to treat harshly, to spoil)
胃	546 page 124	要	729 page 160
背	HAI (to disobey, to rebel); *se*, the back (of a body, a chair, etc.), stature, ridge	訂	TEI (to correct, to establish)
胎	TAI (to conceive; womb, fetus)	計	201 page 55
胞	HŌ (placenta)	変	509 page 116
胆	TAN (liver; spirit, courage)	貞	TEI (right, just, chaste)
臭	SHŪ (smell, stink); *kusa(i)*, ill-smelling, suspicious; ~*kusa(i)*, smelling of ~	負	312 page 77
茶	275 page 70	赴	FU (to go)
草	106 page 36	軌	KI (space between two wheels, print of a wheel)
荒	KŌ; *ara(i)*, violent, rude, wild; *a(reru)*, to become rough, to be dilapidated	軍	593 page 133
荘	SŌ (majestic, solemn; villa)	迷	724 page 159

227

追	280 page 71	面	322 page 79
退	839 page 182	革	746 page 164
送	268 page 68	音	50 page 25
逃	TŌ; *ni(geru)*, to run away, to flee	風	132 page 41
逆	758 page 166	飛	493 page 113
郊	KŌ (suburbs, the country)	食	253 page 65
郎	RŌ (man, male—used as suffix in men's given names)	首	239 page 62
重	245 page 64	香	KŌ, incense; *ka* (lit.), perfume, fragrance
限	601 page 135	点	285 page 72

10 STROKES

| 修 | 633 page 141 | 俳 | HAI (fun, play, humor; actor, actress) |

俵	702 page 155	兼	769 page 168
倉	659 page 146	准	JUN (rule; to imitate, to approve)
個	603 page 135	凍	TŌ; kō(ru), to freeze (v.i.); kogo(eru), to be benumbed with cold
倍	694 page 153	剖	BŌ (to divide, to distinguish)
倒	TŌ; tao(reru), to fall, to break down, to go to ruin; tao(su), to fell, to overthrow	剛	GŌ (inflexible, stubborn, stiff, hard)
候	607 page 136	剤	ZAI (medicine, drug)
借	420 page 99	剣	KEN, tsurugi, sword
倣	HŌ (to model after, to imitate)	勉	317 page 78
値	CHI; ne, price; atai, price, value	匿	TOKU (to give refuge to, to conceal, to hide, to keep secret)
倫	RIN (principles, duty, rules)	原	205 page 56
倹	KEN (frugal, modest, humble)	員	349 page 84

哲	TETSU (wise, sagacious)	宰	SAI (to administer, to manage, to take charge of; chief, head)
唆	SA (to tempt, to instigate)	害	362 page 87
唐	TŌ, Tang (an ancient Chinese dynasty); China (old name used in Japan)	宴	EN, feast, banquet
埋	MAI; u(meru), to bury, to fill up; u(maru), to be buried, to be filled up	家	53 page 25
夏	52 page 25	容	730 page 161
姫	hime, princess, young lady of birth; also used as prefix for "small" or "dainty"	射	SHA; i(ru), to shoot (an arrow, a bird), to strike (one's eyes)
娘	musume, girl, daughter	将	SHŌ (commander; to command; to be about to)
娛	GO (to enjoy, to take pleasure in)	展	847 page 184
娠	SHIN (to conceive, to become pregnant)	峰	HŌ; mine, peak, back (of a sword)
孫	458 page 106	島	292 page 73
宮	374 page 89	差	399 page 94

師	624 page 139	恥	CHI; *haji*, shame, disgrace, humiliation; *ha(jiru)* to be ashamed of
席	444 page 103	恩	558 page 126
帯	669 page 148	恭	KYŌ (respectful, reverent)
座	ZA, seat, gathering, (stand, theater, constellation)	息	454 page 105
庫	206 page 56	悦	ETSU (to be glad, to rejoice)
庭	477 page 110	悟	GO; *sato(ru)*, to be spiritually awakened, to perceive, to comprehend
弱	236 page 62	恵	KEI, E; *megu(mi)*, grace, blessing; *megu(mu)*, to give in charity
徐	JO (slowly, gently)	悩	NŌ; *naya(mi)*, affliction, trouble, pain; *naya(mu)*, to be troubled with
徒	480 page 111	恋	REN; *koi*, love; *koi(shii)*, dear, beloved
従	808 page 176	扇	SEN; *ōgi*, folding fan
恐	KYŌ; *oso(re)*, fear, anxiety; *oso(reru)*, to fear; *oso(roshii)*, fearful, fierce, awful	振	SHIN; *fu(ru)*, to wave (v.t.), to shake (v.t.), to wield; to discard, to jilt

231

捕	HO; *tora(eru)*, to catch, to take hold of	校	75 page 30
捜	SŌ; *saga(su)*, to hunt for, to search for	株	749 page 164
挙	375 page 90	核	KAKU, nucleus, kernel, core, stone (of a fruit)
敏	BIN (clever, quick)	根	216 page 58
料	531 page 121	格	569 page 128
旅	335 page 82	栽	SAI (to plant)
既	KI; *sude(ni)*, already, previously	桃	TŌ; *momo*, peach
時	87 page 32	案	340 page 83
書	92 page 33	桑	SŌ; *kuwa*, mulberry
朕	CHIN, We, Our (formerly used by the Emperor of Japan in Imperial rescripts)	梅	BAI; *ume*, plum, plum tree
朗	RŌ; *hoga(raka)*, fine, cheerful, clear, sonorous	桜	Ō; *sakura*, cherry tree

帰	182 page 51	浸	SHIN; *hita(su)*, to soak, to wet
殉	JUN; *jun(zuru)*, to follow even to death, to sacrifice oneself	消	429 page 100
殊	SHU (especially; to be different)	涙	RUI; *namida*, tear (from the eye)
残	409 page 96	浜	HIN; *hama*, beach, shore
殺	614 page 137	烈	RETSU (valiant, violent, brave, strong)
泰	TAI (peaceful; great, extravagant, extremely)	特	685 page 152
流	334 page 81	珠	SHU (pearl)
浦	HO; *ura*, inlet, beach	班	HAN, squad (mil.), group
浪	RŌ (billow; to wander about)	畔	HAN (vicinity; footpath between rice fields, edge)
浮	FU; *u(ku)*, to float, to be gay, to be left over; *u(kabu)*, to float, to come to mind	留	733 page 161
浴	732 page 161	畜	CHIKU (to raise cattle, to cultivate)

畝	*se*, old unit for measuring land (3.92 sq. rd.)	祥	SHŌ (good fortune, omen)
疲	HI ; *tsuka(re)*, fatigue ; *tsuka(reru)*, to get tired, to become fatigued	租	SO (tribute)
疾	SHITSU (sickness ; to fall ill ; quick, swift)	秩	CHITSU (order, rank)
病	310 page 77	称	815 page 178
症	SHŌ (nature of a disease)	笑	SHŌ ; *wara(i)*, laughter ; *wara(u)*, to laugh, to smile, to chuckle
益	742 page 163	粉	507 page 116
真	438 page 102	粋	SUI, essence, elegance ; delicate, smart, stylish
眠	MIN ; *nemu(ri)*, sleep ; *nemu(ru)*, to sleep	紋	MON, family insignia, crest, figures (in cloth)
砲	HŌ, gun, cannon	納	856 page 186
破	692 page 153	純	810 page 177
秘	HI (to keep secret ; secretly)	紙	85 page 32

紛	FUN; *magi(reru)*, to be obscure, to be diverted, to be confused	脅	KYŌ; *obiya(kasu)*, to threaten, to menace, to intimidate
素	658 page 146	脈	517 page 118
紡	BŌ; *tsumu(gu)*, to spin (thread)	致	CHI (to do, to bring about; taste, appearance)
索	SAKU (cable, rope; to seek for, to search for)	航	396 page 94
翁	Ō, old man, honorific title for an old man	般	HAN (generally; to carry, to turn; to enjoy)
耕	784 page 171	荷	165 page 48
耗	MŌ (to decrease, to spend)	華	KA (flower, blossom; gay, gaudy, colorful, showy)
胴	DŌ, trunk (of the body), body armor	蚊	*ka*, mosquito
胸	KYŌ; *mune*, breast, chest, heart, mind	蚕	617 page 138
能	691 page 153	衰	SUI; *otoro(eru)*, to become weak, to decline
脂	SHI (fat, grease, tallow)	衷	CHŪ (heart, sincerity)

235

被	HI; kōmu(ru), to suffer (damage, etc.), to receive (a favor, etc.)	逐	CHIKU (to chase, to pursue)
討	849 page 184	途	TO (way, road)
訓	764 page 167	通	281 page 71
託	TAKU (to entrust to a person, to make a pretext of)	速	453 page 105
記	180 page 51	造	662 page 147
財	793 page 173	連	538 page 122
貢	KŌ (tribute)	逓	TEI (alternately, by turns; to convey)
起	181 page 51	郡	384 page 91
軒	KEN, suffix for counting houses; noki, eaves	配	299 page 74
辱	JOKU (to put to shame, to disgrace)	酒	422 page 99
透	TŌ (to penetrate); su(ku), to be transparent, to leave a gap, to be thin	針	SHIN; hari, needle, hook, sting (of a bee, etc.), hand (of a clock)

降	KŌ; fu(ru), to fall (rain, snow); o(riru), to get off, to come down, to alight	飢	KI; u(e), hunger, starvation; u(eru), to be hungry, to starve
陛	867 page 188	馬	127 page 40
院	350 page 85	骨	KOTSU; hone, bone, frame
陣	JIN, camp, position (mil.), battle array	高	76 page 30
除	813 page 177	鬼	KI; oni, ogre, fiend, demon
陥	KAN; ochii(ru), to fall into, to yield, to cave in, to fall (to surrender to a siege)	党	848 page 184
隻	SEKI, suffix for counting ships		

11 STROKES

乾	KAN (to dry, to be thirsty)	健	599 page 134
偏	HEN (to be one-sided, to be partial)	側	667 page 148
停	476 page 110	偶	GŪ (even number; by chance, accidentally)

偽	GI; *itsuwa(ru)*, to tell a lie, to pretend, to deceive	域	IKI (boundary, border, end, limits)
剰	JŌ (surplus; moreover)	執	SHITSU, SHŪ; *to-(ru)*, to do (business, etc.), to manage, to take, to grasp
副	709 page 156	培	BAI (to cultivate)
動	296 page 74	基	755 page 166
勘	KAN, perception, intuition	堂	486 page 112
務	722 page 159	婆	BA (old woman, old mother)
唯	YUI (merely, only, alone)	婚	KON (marriage)
唱	430 page 101	婦	707 page 156
商	431 page 101	宿	634 page 141
問	520 page 119	寂	JAKU; *sabi(shii)*, lonesome, lonely, solitary
啓	KEI (to enlighten, to open)	寄	576 page 130

238

密	MITSU, dense, secret, (close, minute)	強	192 page 53
尉	I (military rank)	彩	SAI (coloration; to color)
崇	SŪ (lofty, noble; to respect, to worship)	彫	CHŌ; ho(ru), to carve, to engrave
崩	HŌ (to crumble, to collapse, to change for the worse, to be destroyed)	得	850 page 185
巣	SŌ; su, nest, lair, den, cobweb, beehive	御	GYO, GO; on, honorific prefix; gyo(suru), to drive (a horse)
帳	470 page 109	患	KAN (sickness, anxiety, trouble)
常	642 page 143	悼	TŌ (to mourn over, to lament, to feel pity for)
庶	SHO (various, all, many)	情	643 page 143
康	608 page 136	惜	SEKI; o(shii), regrettable; precious; wasteful; o(shimu), to begrudge, to regret
庸	YŌ (moderate, ordinary, mediocre)	悪	152 page 45
張	675 page 150	惨	SAN (cruel, horrible, appalling)

捨	SHA; *su(teru)*, to throw away, to abandon	措	SO (to put aside, to except, to dispose of; to place)
掃	SŌ; *ha(ku)*, to sweep	描	BYŌ; *ega(ku)*, to picture, to describe
授	803 page 175	掲	KEI; *kaka(geru)*, to put up, to hoist, to carry
排	HAI (to reject; to display, to push open)	教	191 page 53
掘	KUTSU; *ho(ru)*, to dig, to dig up	救	584 page 131
掛	*ka(keru)*, to hang (v.t.), to sit on (a chair, etc.), to cover with	敗	693 page 153
採	791 page 173	斜	SHA; *nana(me)*, slanting, oblique
探	TAN; *sagu(ru)*, to spy into, to search, to feel after, to fathom	断	841 page 183
接	652 page 145	旋	SEN (to rotate, to return)
控	KŌ; *hika(eru)*, to write down; to refrain from, to be moderate in, to wait	族	455 page 106
推	821 page 179	望	514 page 117

械	360 page 87	渇	KATSU, thirst; (to be thirsty, to dry up)
欲	876 page 190	渋	JŪ; *shibu*, astringent juice; *shibu(i)*, astringent, tasteful, refined, sober, glum
渉	SHŌ (to wade, to cross over, to walk about; to be related to)	済	792 page 173
液	552 page 125	猛	MŌ (strong, valiant, brave, fierce, wild)
涼	RYŌ (lit.), coolness; *suzu(shii)*, cool	猟	RYŌ, hunting, shooting
淑	SHUKU (graceful, gentle)	率	878 page 190
淡	TAN; *awa(i)*, light (color, taste, etc.), transitory (love, joy, etc.)	現	602 page 135
深	258 page 66	球	188 page 52
混	787 page 172	理	333 page 81
清	440 page 103	産	408 page 96
添	TEN; *so(eru)*, to annex (to), to add (to), to garnish (cooking)	略	879 page 190

異	738 page 162	符	FU (tally, mark, sign, good omen, charm, talisman)
盛	SEI, JŌ (prosperous); *saka(ri)*, prime, heyday; *mo(ru)*, to dish up, to heap up	第	273 page 69
盗	TŌ; *nusu(mu)*, to steal, to rob	粒	RYŪ; *tsubu*, grain, drop
眼	754 page 165	粗	SO (rough, loose, coarse, humble)
票	703 page 155	粘	NEN; *neba(ru)*, to be sticky; to persevere
祭	400 page 95	紫	SHI; *murasaki*, purple, violet
移	547 page 124	累	RUI, trouble, involvement; (to pile up, to trouble; to be acquainted with)
窒	CHITSU (to block up, to obstruct; nitrogen)	細	218 page 58
窓	SŌ; *mado*, window	紳	SHIN (ceremonial sash; man of high birth)
章	432 page 101	紹	SHŌ (to introduce a person; to succeed to)
笛	TEKI; *fue*, flute	紺	KON, dark blue

終	241 page 63	菊	KIKU, chrysanthe-mum
組	103 page 35	菌	KIN, germ, fungus
経	596 page 134	菓	KA (fruit, nut, ber-ry)
翌	YOKU (the next~, the following~; used before "day," "morn-ing," "year," etc.)	菜	401 page 95
習	426 page 100	著	843 page 183
粛	SHUKU (to be re-spectful, to be mod-est, to admonish, to be severe)	虚	KYO, KO (empty, vain)
脚	KYAKU (leg, lower part, position), suffix for counting legged furniture	術	636 page 142
脱	DATSU (to omit, to escape); nu(gu), to take off (shoes, coat, etc.)	袋	TAI; fukuro, bag, sack, pouch
脳	NŌ, brain, brains	規	577 page 130
舶	HAKU (ocean-going ship)	視	798 page 174
船	266 page 68	訟	SHŌ (to sue, to go to law)

訪	HŌ; *otozu(reru)*, to visit, to call on (at)	軟	NAN (soft, weak, feeble)
設	653 page 145	転	479 page 110
許	587 page 132	逮	TAI (to catch, to arrest, to overtake, to pursue)
訳	874 page 189	週	242 page 63
豚	TON; *buta*, pig	進	259 page 66
貧	705 page 156	逸	ITSU (to excel, to be lost, to be rash, to run off, to enjoy oneself)
貨	357 page 86	部	504 page 115
販	HAN (to sell, to deal in)	郭	KAKU (enclosure, red-light district)
貫	KAN, old unit of weight (8.27 lb.); *tsuranu(ku)*, to pierce, to carry out, to attain	郵	YŪ (collection and delivery of goods, letters, etc.; post town)
責	649 page 144	都	287 page 72
赦	SHA (to forgive, to pardon)	郷	KYŌ, GŌ (the country, village, one's native place)

酔	SUI; *yo(u)*, to get drunk, to become sick (sea, car, air), to be in ecstasy	険	770 page 169
釈	802 page 175	雪	100 page 35
野	323 page 79	頂	CHŌ (to receive); *itadaki*, summit, top
閉	HEI; *to(jiru)*, to shut, to close	魚	190 page 53
陪	BAI (to attend upon; attendant)	鳥	117 page 38
陰	IN, gloom, negative, the female principle (yin); *kage*, shadow, shade, back	麻	MA; *asa*, hemp, flax
陳	CHIN (to state, to display; to be old)	黄	214 page 57
陵	RYŌ; *misasagi*, Imperial mausoleum	黒	80 page 31
陶	TŌ (pottery, porcelain)	斉	SAI (religious purification; a room)
陸	529 page 120	隆	RYŪ (high, prosperous, flourishing)

12 STROKES

偉	I; *era(i)*, great, admirable	喚	KAN (to call, to cry, to summon)
傍	BŌ (side, neighborhood)	喜	370 page 89
備	700 page 155	喪	SŌ (to lose, to ruin); *mo*, mourning
割	KATSU; *wa(ru)*, to divide, to separate, to split, to dilute; *wari*, rate, percentage	喫	KITSU (to eat, to drink)
創	832 page 181	圏	KEN, sphere, range
勝	250 page 65	堅	KEN; *kata(i)*, hard, tough, tight, firm, solid, strict, sound
募	BO; *tsuno(ru)*, to collect, to raise (troops, etc.); to grow intense	堤	TEI; *tsutsumi*, bank (of a river, etc.)
勤	762 page 167	堪	KAN; *ta(eru)*, to endure, to bear, to withstand, to resist
博	695 page 154	報	717 page 158
善	831 page 181	場	252 page 65

246

堕	DA (to fall, to get into, to let fall, to lose)	属	835 page 182
塔	TŌ, tower, pagoda, steeple	帽	BŌ (headgear, head-dress)
塁	RUI, base (in base-ball), fort	幅	FUKU, scroll, suffix for counting scrolls; *haba*, width, differ-ence in price
奥	OKU, interior, depths, heart; Ō (interior)	幾	KI; *iku~*, how many?, how much?, some (used as prefix)
婿	SEI; *muko*, son-in-law, bridegroom	廊	RŌ (corridor, pas-sage)
媒	BAI (intermediation, matchmaking, inter-mediary, go-between)	廃	HAI (to go out of use or fashion, to be abolished, to decline)
富	864 page 187	弾	DAN (bullet, ball; to investigate; to play on a musical instru-ment)
寒	175 page 50	復	710 page 157
尊	838 page 182	循	JUN (to obey, to observe, to follow; to revolve)
尋	JIN; *tazu(neru)*, to ask, to look for	悲	494 page 113
就	807 page 176	惑	WAKU; *mado(u)*, to be puzzled, to go astray, to be capti-vated by

247

惰	DA (to be idle, to neglect)	敢	KAN (daringly, boldly)
愉	YU (to rejoice, to enjoy oneself)	散	407 page 96
慌	KŌ (busy, bustling; to be flurried, to lose one's presence of mind)	敬	766 page 168
掌	SHŌ (palm of the hand; to control, to preside over)	晩	BAN (late), evening, night
提	845 page 184	普	FU (wide, universal, general)
揚	YŌ; a(geru), to raise, to send up, to hoist; to fry	景	386 page 92
換	KAN; ka(eru), to exchange, to change (v. t.); ka(waru), to change (v. i.)	晴	265 page 68
握	AKU; nigi(ru), to grasp, to clasp, to hold, to seize	晶	SHŌ (bright; crystal)
援	EN (to help, to rescue, to pull)	暑	247 page 64
揮	(to wield, to display, to command)	暁	GYŌ; akatsuki, dawn, daybreak
揺	YŌ; yu(reru), to shake (v. i.), to swing, to flicker	替	TAI; ka(eru), to exchange, to substitute, to convert

最	402 page 95	款	KAN (sincerity, good-will; article in a legal document)
朝	118 page 38	殖	SHOKU (to increase, to grow up, to plant)
期	183 page 51	減	775 page 170
棋	KI (chessman, Japanese chess)	渡	TO; wata(ru), to go over, to be imported, to change hands, to migrate
棒	BŌ, stick, club	測	668 page 148
森	41 page 23	港	397 page 94
棺	KAN, casket, coffin	湖	394 page 93
植	435 page 102	湯	482 page 111
極	382 page 91	温	162 page 47
検	771 page 169	滋	JI (nourishing; to flourish, to be luxuriant)
欺	GI; azamu(ku), to deceive, to cheat	満	721 page 159

249

湿	SHITSU; *shime(ru)*, to become damp, to moisten	畳	JŌ, suffix for counting mats; *tatami*, mat
湾	WAN, bay, gulf	疎	SO (to be estranged; to know little of; to be sparse)
無	723 page 159	痘	TŌ (smallpox)
焦	SHŌ (to pine for); *ko(geru)*, to scorch, to burn (v. i.); *ko(gasu)*, to burn (v. t.)	痛	TSŪ; *ita(mi)*, pain; *ita(mu)*, to feel pain, to ache
然	450 page 105	痢	RI (diarrhoea)
煮	SHA; *ni(ru)*, to cook (v. t.)	登	483 page 111
焼	434 page 101	短	466 page 108
営	741 page 163	硝	SHŌ (niter, gunpowder)
猶	YŪ (to hesitate; moreover, even, still; as if)	硫	RYŪ (sulfur)
琴	KIN; *koto*, Japanese harp	硬	KŌ (hard, tough, stiff, firm)
番	306 page 76	税	826 page 180

程	846 page 184	絞	KŌ; *shibo(ru)*, to wring, to squeeze, to extort, to scold; *shi-(meru)*, to strangle
童	487 page 112	絡	RAKU (to twine a-round, to surround)
筆	701 page 155	給	585 page 132
等	484 page 111	統	682 page 151
筋	KIN; *suji*, sinew, plot (of a story), source, logic, lineage, stripe, line, vein	絵	172 page 49
筒	TŌ; *tsutsu*, pipe, tube	着	276 page 70
答	293 page 73	脹	CHŌ (to swell)
策	795 page 174	腕	WAN; *ude*, arm, talent, ability
粧	SHŌ (to paint and powder, to embellish)	落	330 page 81
結	390 page 93	葉	327 page 80
絶	828 page 180	葬	SŌ; *hōmu(ru)*, to bury, to consign to oblivion, to shelve

蛮	BAN (barbarian)	詐	SA (to tell a lie, to pretend, to deceive)
衆	806 page 176	詔	SHŌ; *mikotonori*, Imperial edict
街	GAI, street, avenue (used as suffix)	評	863 page 187
裁	SAI (to judge, to decide); *ta(tsu)*, to cut (cloth, etc.)	詞	799 page 174
裂	RETSU; *sa(ku)*, to tear, to rend (v. t.); *sa(keru)*, to tear, to rend (v. i.)	詠	EI, poem, ode, recitation of poetry
裕	YŪ (abundant, broad-minded, at ease)	証	816 page 178
補	868 page 188	象	663 page 147
装	SŌ, SHŌ; *yoso-o(i)*, dress, decoration; *yoso-o(u)*, to dress, to adorn, to pretend	貯	674 page 149
覚	363 page 87	貴	756 page 166
訴	SO; *utta(e)*, lawsuit, appeal, complaint; *utta(eru)*, to sue, to resort to, to appeal	買	300 page 75
診	SHIN (to examine, to diagnose)	貸	670 page 149

費	495 page 114	運	157 page 46
貿	719 page 158	遍	HEN (wide, universal)
賀	565 page 128	過	562 page 127
超	CHŌ, super- (used as prefix); (to exceed, to surpass, to jump over, to go over)	道	122 page 39
越	ETSU; ko(eru), to go over, to exceed; ko-(su), to cross, to exceed, to move (to)	達	465 page 108
距	KYO (to separate, to be distant, to reach)	遅	CHI (late, slow); oku-(reru), to be late
軸	JIKU, axis, axle, scroll picture, holder, stalk	酢	SAKU; su, vinegar
軽	387 page 92	量	734 page 161
遂	SUI (at last); to(geru), to accomplish, to attain	鈍	DON; nibu(i), dull, slow, blunt, dim
遇	GŪ (to treat, to deal with, to meet with, to come across)	開	171 page 49
遊	326 page 80	閑	KAN (quiet, tranquil; leisure, time to spare)

253

間	58 page 26	雇	KO; *yato(u)*, to hire, to employ
陽	527 page 120	雲	47 page 24
隊	462 page 107	項	KŌ, clause, paragraph, item
階	361 page 87	順	427 page 100
随	ZUI (to follow, to accompany; freely; as one pleases)	飲	351 page 85
雄	YŪ (strong, valiant, brave, surpassing); *osu, o*, male animal	飯	696 page 154
雅	GA (elegant, graceful)	歯	414 page 97
集	243 page 63		

13 STROKES

| 傑 | KETSU (to excel, to surpass; man of great caliber) | 債 | SAI (debt, loan) |
| 催 | SAI; *moyo-o(shi)*, meeting, auspices; *moyo-o(su)*, to hold (a meeting), to feel | 傷 | SHŌ (to hurt, to spoil, to worry); *kizu*, wound, injury |

傾	KEI; *katamu(ki)*, inclination; *katamu(ku)* (v. i.), *katamu(keru)* (v. t.), to incline	墓	869 page 188
働	488 page 112	夢	MU; *yume*, dream, vision, transiency
僧	SŌ, Buddhist priest, bonze	奨	SHŌ (to encourage, to promote)
勢	441 page 103	嫁	KA; *yome*, daughter-in-law, young wife, bride
勧	752 page 165	寝	SHIN; *ne(ru)*, to go to bed, to sleep, to lie down
嗣	SHI (to succeed to, to inherit; heir, successor)	寛	KAN (generous, easy)
嘆	TAN; *nage(ku)*, to bewail, to deplore, to sigh	幕	BAKU; MAKU, curtain, screen, hangings; act (of a play, opera, etc.)
園	159 page 46	幹	751 page 165
塊	KAI (clod, lump)	廉	REN (noble, lofty, pure; cheap)
塑	SO (earthen figure)	微	BI (slight, little, faint, dim)
塗	TO; *nu(ru)*, to paint, to plaster, to coat, to lacquer, to smear	想	660 page 147

愁	SHŪ (grief, sorrow, distress)	携	KEI; *tazusa(eru)*, to carry in one's hand, to take with one
意	155 page 46	搾	SAKU (to squeeze, to compress)
愚	GU; *oro(ka)*, foolish, stupid, silly	摂	SETSU (to take, to cultivate, to act in place of)
愛	339 page 82	数	262 page 67
感	176 page 50	新	256 page 66
慎	SHIN; *tsutsushi(mu)*, to be discreet, to refrain from	暇	KA; *hima*, time, leisure, dismissal
慈	JI (to love, to cherish, to pity)	暖	DAN; *atata(kai)*, warm, cordial
慨	GAI (to deplore, to lament)	暗	154 page 45
戦	448 page 104	棄	KI (to throw away, to abandon, to reject)
損	837 page 182	業	380 page 91
搬	HAN (to carry, to transport, to remove)	楽	331 page 81

楼	RŌ (lit.), stately mansion with two or more stories, watchtower	煙	EN; *kemuri*, smoke
歳	SAI, ~ years old (used as suffix); SEI (year, age, time)	照	433 page 101
殿	TEN, DEN; ~*dono*, Mr., Mrs., etc. (used in formal letters); *tono*, lord, my lord	煩	HAN, trouble, worry; *wazura(washii)*, complicated, troublesome
源	GEN; *minamoto*, origin, source	献	KEN, KON (to dedicate, to offer, to present)
準	637 page 142	痴	CHI (foolish, stupid)
溶	YŌ; *to(keru)*, to melt, to dissolve (v. i.); *to(kasu)*, to melt (v. t.)	盟	873 page 189
滅	METSU; *horo(biru)*, to go to ruin, to die out; *horo(bosu)*, to ruin, to destroy	睡	SUI (to sleep, to doze)
滑	KATSU (smooth, even; to slide)	督	TOKU (to control, to supervise, to urge)
滞	TAI; *todokō(ru)*, to stagnate, to fall into arrears, to be left undone	碁	GO, the Japanese game of *go*
漢	572 page 129	禁	763 page 167
滝	*taki*, waterfall, cataract, cascade	禍	KA (misfortune, disaster, evil)

福	506 page 116	義	580 page 131
禅	ZEN, Dhyāna, the Zen sect of Buddhism, religious meditation	聖	824 page 179
稚	CHI (infant, young, childish, raw)	腰	YŌ; *koshi*, waist, loins
節	446 page 104	腸	676 page 150
絹	772 page 169	腹	FUKU; *hara*, belly, abdomen, guts; heart, mind
継	KEI; *tsu(gi)* a patch; *tsu(gu)*, to inherit, to succeed to, to come into (property, etc.)	艇	TEI (boat)
続	456 page 106	蒸	JŌ; *mu(su)*, to steam, to foment, to be sultry or sweltering
罪	794 page 173	蓄	CHIKU (to store, to save)
置	469 page 108	虜	RYO (captive, prisoner of war)
署	SHO, station (police, fire, etc.), suffix for " government office "	虞	*osore*, anxiety, apprehension
群	594 page 133	裏	RI; *ura*, reverse side, back, opposite, second half (baseball)

裸	RA; *hadaka*, nakedness, nude	誉	YO; *homa(re)*, honor, credit, glory, reputation
解	567 page 128	豊	870 page 189
触	SHOKU; *fu(reru)*, to touch, to mention; to conflict with; to proclaim	債	844 page 183
試	416 page 98	賄	WAI (wealth, bribe; to cater for)
詩	415 page 98	資	800 page 175
詰	KITSU (to call to account); *tsu(meru)*, to cram, to put close to, to shorten	賊	ZOKU, thief, robber, burglar
話	151 page 45	跡	SEKI; *ato*, mark, trace, trail, wake, ruins
該	GAI, that, the very, the ~ in question (used as prefix)	路	540 page 123
詳	SHŌ; *kuwa(shii)*, detailed, minute; well-informed	跳	CHŌ (to jump, to leap, to flee)
誇	KO; *hoko(ri)*, pride; *hoko(ru)*, to be proud of, to boast of	践	SEN (to step on, to go, to carry out)
誠	825 page 180	較	KAKU (to compare)

載	SAI; *no(seru)*, to load, to place (on); to put on record, to publish	鉱	610 page 137
辞	626 page 140	隔	KAKU; *heda(teru)*, to separate, to screen, to estrange; *heda(taru)*, to be distant from
農	491 page 113	雌	SHI; *mesu, me*, female (animal, bird; *me* is also used in the case of plants)
違	I; *chiga(u)*, to differ from, to be wrong	零	REI, zero, (to fall, to rain; fragment)
遠	160 page 47	雷	RAI; *kaminari*, thunder, thunderbolt
遣	KEN (to send, to dispatch, to bestow)	電	286 page 72
酬	SHŪ (to reward, to recompense, to return, to repay)	預	875 page 190
酪	RAKU (dairy products)	頒	HAN (to distribute, to divide)
鈴	REI; RIN, *suzu*, small bell	飼	SHI; *ka(u)*, to raise, to rear, to keep (animals)
鉛	EN; *namari*, lead (metal)	飽	HŌ; *a(ki)*, weariness, tiresomeness; *a(kiru)*, to grow tired of, to become weary of
鉄	283 page 71	飾	SHOKU; *kaza(ru)*, to ornament, to embellish, to exhibit, to affect

塩	354 page 85	鼓	KO; *tsuzumi*, hand drum

14 STROKES

像	664 page 147	寧	NEI (quiet, peaceful, easy; kind; rather)
僚	RYŌ (an official; friend, colleague)	層	SŌ, stratum, layer; (to be piled up)
境	761 page 167	彰	SHŌ (manifest, clear; to elucidate)
増	665 page 148	徴	CHŌ (symptom, sign; effect, proof; to summon)
墨	BOKU; *sumi*, India ink, ink stick	徳	851 page 185
奪	DATSU; *uba(u)*, to take by force, to rob, to captivate	態	840 page 183
嫡	CHAKU (heir, legitimate child)	慕	BO; *shita(u)*, to yearn for, to adore, to follow
察	406 page 96	慢	MAN (to be idle, to neglect; to despise, to be haughty, to be selfish)
寡	KA (few, little, small, scanty; alone; widow)	慣	574 page 129

憎	ZŌ; *niku(mu)*, to hate, to detest	滴	TEKI (drop of liquid, trickle; to drip); suffix for counting drops of liquid
摘	TEKI (to disclose, to reveal, to point out); *tsu(mu)*, to pick, to pluck	漁	588 page 132
旗	371 page 89	漂	HYŌ (to wander about; to bleach); *tadayo(u)*, to drift, to float
暮	BO; *ku(re)*, year end; *ku(reru)*, to grow dark, to end; *ku(rasu)*, to live, to make a living	漆	SHITSU; *urushi*, lacquer
暦	REKI; *koyomi*, calendar, almanac	漏	RŌ; *mo(ru)*, to leak; *mo(reru)*, to leak, to get out (secret, etc.), to be omitted
構	785 page 172	演	553 page 125
概	GAI (roughly, generally, as a rule)	漫	MAN (in spite of oneself, involuntarily, self-willfulness; vast, wide, lax)
模	MO, BO (model, mold; to model after)	漸	ZEN (gradually; to advance gradually; at last)
様	328 page 80	獄	GOKU, prison, jail
歌	166 page 48	疑	757 page 166
歴	536 page 122	碑	HI, monument, tombstone

262

磁	JI (magnet, compass; porcelain)	綱	KŌ (basic principles); *tsuna*, rope, cable; last hope (of life, etc.)
種	423 page 99	網	MŌ; *ami*, net, netting
稲	TŌ; *ine*, rice plant	綿	725 page 160
穀	786 page 172	緒	SHO, beginning, (lineage; clue); *o*, cord, string (of a musical instrument)
端	TAN (right, correct, just); *hashi*, end, tip, edge, border	練	539 page 122
箇	KA (used as auxiliary in counting)	総	661 page 147
算	219 page 58	罰	BATSU, penalty, punishment; *bas-(suru)*, to punish, to penalize
管	573 page 129	聞	314 page 77
精	647 page 144	腐	FU; *kusa(ru)*, to go bad, to rot; to be dejected, to lose heart
緑	532 page 121	膜	MAKU, membrane
維	I (to keep; to fasten; fundamental principles)	製	648 page 144

複	865 page 188	踊	YŌ; *odo(ri)*, dance; *odo(ru)*, to dance, to jump
誌	SHI (record; to write down)	適	679 page 150
認	855 page 186	遭	SŌ (to encounter, to come across)
誓	SEI; *chika(i)*, oath, vow; *chika(u)*, to swear, to take a vow	酵	KŌ (yeast, ferment, saké lees)
誕	TAN (to be born; to give birth to)	酷	KOKU, severity, cruelty, harshness
誘	YŪ; *saso(i)*, invitation, temptation; *saso(u)*, to invite, to induce, to allure	酸	618 page 138
語	209 page 56	銀	196 page 54
誤	779 page 170	銃	JŪ, gun, rifle
説	654 page 145	銅	683 page 151
読	123 page 39	銑	SEN (pig iron)
豪	GŌ (to excel, to stand pre-eminent; strong, vigorous)	銘	MEI, signature, inscription, appellation, motto, (to inscribe)

錢	656 page 146	靜	442 page 103
閣	KAKU (mansion, palace, tower; government office)	領	735 page 162
閥	BATSU, clique, faction, clan	駆	KU (to drive a vehicle, to chase); *ka(keru)*, to run, to gallop
関	365 page 88	駅	158 page 46
際	612 page 137	髮	HATSU; *kami*, hair, hairdo
障	SHŌ (to hinder, to interfere with)	魂	KON; *tamashii*, soul, spirit, ghost
隱	IN; *kaku(reru)*, to hide (v.i.), to disappear; *kaku(su)*, to hide (v.t.), to conceal	鳴	321 page 79
雜	615 page 138	鼻	496 page 114
需	804 page 175		

15 STROKES

| 儀 | GI, rule, ceremony, affair, matter | 億 | 557
page 126 |

265

劇	GEKI, drama, play, (intense, violent, severe, hard)	幣	HEI (pendant paper strips in a Shinto shrine; riches, offering, money)
勲	KUN (meritorious deed, distinguished service)	弊	HEI, evil, abuse, vice; our (used as prefix denoting modesty)
器	372 page 89	影	EI; *kage*, shadow, reflection, image, phantom, light
噴	FUN (to emit, to belch, to send forth)	徹	TETSU (to pierce, to penetrate)
嘱	SHOKU (to entrust, to request)	慮	RYO (to consider, to deliberate, to plan, to be anxious)
墜	TSUI (to fall, to drop)	慰	I; *nagusa(me)*, comfort; *nagusa(mi)*, pastime; *nagusa(meru)*, to comfort, to console
墳	FUN (mound, tumulus, hillock, tomb)	慶	KEI (congratulation, happiness; to rejoice)
審	SHIN (detailed, full, clear, evident, obvious)	憂	YŪ; *ure(i)*, grief, anxiety, affliction; *ure-(eru)*, to fear, to lament, to be worried
寮	RYŌ, boarding house, dormitory	憤	FUN; *ikidō(ru)*, to be indignant, to resent
導	684 page 151	戯	GI (fun, play, flirtation); *tawamu(reru)*, to joke, to play, to flirt with
履	RI (footwear; to walk; to do, to experience)	摩	MA (to rub, to grind, to wear away); *ma-(suru)* (lit.), to nearly touch; to scrape

撤	TETSU; *tes(suru)*, to remove, to get rid of, to withdraw (an army, etc.)	歓	753 page 165
撮	SATSU (to pinch, to pick, to gather; to take a photograph)	潔	767 page 168
撲	BOKU (to strike, to beat)	潜	SEN (to dive into water; secretly); *hiso-(mu)*, to conceal oneself, to lurk
撃	GEKI; *u(tsu)*, to fire (a gun, etc.), to attack, to strike, to fight	潤	JUN; *uruo(i)*, moisture; profit; charm; *uruo(su)* (v. t.), to moisten; to profit
敵	678 page 150	潮	CHŌ; *shio*, tide, sea water; opportunity
敷	FU; *shi(ku)*, to spread, to pave, to sit on (a cushion), to lay (a railway)	澄	CHŌ; *su(mu)*, to become clear or serene (moon, stream, sky, mind, etc.)
暫	ZAN (for a little while, for some time)	熟	JUKU (carefully, attentively); *juku(suru)*, to grow ripe, to mature
暴	871 page 189	熱	490 page 113
標	704 page 155	監	KAN (to watch over, to keep control over, to supervise; prison, jail)
横	355 page 86	盤	BAN, board (for chess, etc.), (shallow basin, phonograph record, plate)
権	774 page 169	確	570 page 129

稿	KŌ, draft, rough copy, manuscript	緩	KAN (slow, easy, slack, lenient)
穂	SUI; *ho*, ear (of wheat, etc.), head	罷	HI (to pause, to intermit, to dismiss, to release, to get tired)
窮	KYŪ; *kiwa(meru)*, to carry to extremes; *kiwa(maru)*, to end, to reach the extreme	膚	FU; *hada*, skin (of the body)
窯	YŌ (kiln for baking tiles, ceramics, etc.)	舗	HO (store; to pave)
箱	*hako*, box, case	舞	BU; *mai*, dancing, dance; *ma(u)*, to dance
範	HAN, example, model	蔵	833 page 181
緊	KIN (to shrink, to become tight, to contract; severe, strict, hard, solid)	衝	SHŌ, important position, focus; (to attack, to strike against; to brave)
線	447 page 104	課	564 page 127
締	TEI; *shi(maru)*, to be shut, to be tight; *shi(meru)*, to tie, to tighten, to shut (v.t.)	調	471 page 109
縁	EN, relation, ties, blood relation; fate; veranda, porch; *fuchi*, edge, verge	談	467 page 108
編	714 page 157	請	SEI, SHIN; *ko(u)*, to beg, to ask, to request; *u(keru)*, to receive, to undertake

論	881 page 191	趣	SHU; *omomuki*, taste, elegance, grace, air, appearance, purport, effect
諸	812 page 177	踏	TŌ; *fu(mu)*, to step on, to tread on
諾	DAKU, consent, assent	輝	KI; *kagaya(ku)*, to shine, to be radiant
謁	ETSU, (Imperial) audience; audience with persons of high rank	輩	HAI (fellows, companions)
賓	HIN (guest)	輪	533 page 121
賜	SHI; *tama(waru)*, to deign to give, to grant, to award	導	JUN (to obey, to observe, to abide by)
賞	641 page 143	遷	SEN (to move from one location to another, to transfer)
賠	BAI (to make up for, to compensate for)	選	449 page 104
賦	FU (lit.), ode, poetical prose; tribute, levy, allotment	遺	739 page 162
質	628 page 140	鋭	EI; *surudo(i)*, sharp, pointed, biting, acute, keen, smart
賛	619 page 138	鋳	CHŪ; *i(ru)*, to cast (metal), to found

閲	ETSU (lit.), inspection, examination; (to examine, to inspect, to peruse, to elapse)	餓	GA (to be hungry, to starve)
震	SHIN; *furu(u)*, *furu(eru)*, to shake (v. i.), to tremble; *furu(waseru)*, to shake (v. t.)	駐	CHŪ (to stop, to stay)
霊	REI, soul, spirit, ghost	魅	MI; *mi(suru)* (lit.), to fascinate, to enchant, to bewitch
養	731 page 161	黙	MOKU; *dama(ru)*, to become silent, to close one's lips

16 STROKES

儒	JU (Confucianism, Confucianist, scholar; cowardice, tenderness)	奮	866 page 188
凝	GYŌ; *ko(ri)*, stiffness; *ko(ru)*, to be absorbed in, to elaborate, to grow stiff	嬢	JŌ, Miss (used as suffix), (girl, unmarried lady, daughter)
墾	KON (to cultivate, to farm, to reclaim)	憩	KEI (to take a rest)
壁	HEKI; *kabe*, wall	憲	773 page 169
壇	DAN, platform, dais, raised floor	憶	OKU (to remember, to keep in mind, to think)
壊	KAI (to collapse, to be destroyed; to break, to destroy)	憾	KAN (to regret, to be sorry for)

懐	KAI (one's pocket; to think, to long for)	燃	690 page 153
擁	YŌ; *yō(suru)*, to protect, to embrace, to hold	燈	485 page 112
操	SŌ (to handle, to manage, to manipulate); *misao*, chastity, virtue, constancy	獲	KAKU; *e(ru)*, to get, to obtain, to gain
整	443 page 103	獣	JŪ; *kemono*, beast, brute
曇	DON; *kumo(ri)*, cloudy weather, blur; *kumo(ru)*, to become cloudy, to become dim	積	445 page 104
樹	JU (living tree, vegetation; to stand, to plant)	穏	ON; *oda(yaka)*, calm, quiet, peaceful, mild
橋	193 page 53	築	673 page 149
機	373 page 89	篤	TOKU (genuine, sincere, hearty, cordial)
激	GEKI; *geki(suru)*, to be excited or enraged; *hage(shii)*, violent, intense, passionate	糖	TŌ (sugar)
濁	DAKU; *nigo(ri)*, turbidity; voiced sound; *nigo(ru)*, to become muddy or cloudy	緯	I (parallels of latitude; cross-threads)
濃	NŌ; *ko(i)*, dark, deep, thick, heavy, strong	縛	BAKU; *shiba(ru)*, to bind, to tie, to arrest

縫	HŌ; *nu(u)*, to sew, to stitch	衛	551 page 125
縦	JŪ; *tate*, vertical direction, length, height	衡	KŌ (scale beam; to measure, to weigh)
繁	HAN (thick, many, much, thriving; troublesome, busy, mixed)	親	260 page 67
膨	BŌ (to swell, to expand)	諭	YU (to admonish)
興	589 page 132	諮	SHI (to consult, to ask counsel of)
薄	HAKU; *usu(i)*, thin, light, pale, weak, small (profit, etc.)	謀	BŌ (plan, device, stratagem, plot)
薦	SEN (to recommend)	謡	YŌ; *utai*, chanting of a *Noh* drama text
薪	SHIN (firewood)	賢	KEN; *kashiko(i)*, wise, intelligent, tactful, smart, shrewd
薫	KUN, (fragrance; to be fragrant)	頼	RAI; *tano(mi)*, request, recourse; *tano(mu)*, to ask, to entrust with, to rely on
薬	521 page 119	輸	727 page 160
融	YŪ (to melt; to circulate, to ventilate)	避	HI; *sa(keru)*, to avoid, to keep away from, to shirk

還	KAN (to return, to come back)	錬	REN (to temper or forge metal; to train, to cultivate, to polish, to drill morally)
鋼	KŌ, steel	隣	RIN; *tonari*, next-door house; next to, neighboring
録	543 page 123	隷	REI (servant, follower)
錘	SUI (weight for scales, sinker for fishing line); *tsumu*, spindle	頭	294 page 73
錠	JŌ, lock, padlock; tablet (medical) (used as suffix for counting tablets)	館	366 page 88
錯	SAKU (to be mixed together, to make a mistake)		

17 STROKES

償	SHŌ; *tsuguna(i)*, indemnity, atonement; *tsuguna(u)*, to make up for, to atone for	懇	KON (kind, cordial, in love with, intimate)
優	YŪ, excellent; *yasa-(shii)*, gentle, tender, kind, affectionate, graceful	擦	SATSU (to rub, to scrub, to scratch)
嚇	KAKU (to threaten, to menace)	擬	GI; *gi(suru)*, to point or aim (an object) at; to imitate; to compare
厳	776 page 170	燥	SŌ (to dry)

爵	SHAKU (peerage, title and court rank)	謄	TŌ (to take a copy of, to transcribe)
犠	GI (sacrifice, victim)	謙	KEN (to humble oneself, to condescend)
環	KAN (ring, link; to surround)	講	609 page 136
療	RYŌ (to cure, to heal)	謝	630 page 141
礁	SHŌ (submerged rock, unknown reef)	謹	KIN (to restrain oneself, to be respectful)
縮	SHUKU; *chiji(mu)* (v.i.), *chiji(meru)* (v.t.), to shrink, to contract, to draw in	購	KŌ (to purchase, to buy)
績	650 page 145	轄	KATSU (control, management)
繊	SEN (thin, slender, fine, small)	醜	SHŪ; *miniku(i)*, ugly, unseemly, ignoble
翼	YOKU (to aid, to assist); *tsubasa*, wing	鍛	TAN; *kita(eru)*, to forge; to train, to cultivate (morally)
聴	CHŌ (to listen to, to comply with)	霜	SŌ; *shimo*, frost
覧	RAN (to see, to look at)	鮮	SEN (Korea; fresh, newly produced, vivid, bright, splendid; few, little)

| 齢 | REI (age, years) | | |

18 STROKES

懲	CHŌ; ko(rasu), to punish, to discipline, to chasten	織	644 page 143
曜	329 page 80	繕	ZEN; tsukuro(u), to patch up, to mend, to trim, to smooth over
濫	RAN (at random, wantonly; excessive; to overflow, to float)	繭	KEN; mayu, silk-worm cocoon
癖	HEKI; kuse, habit, peculiar way, friz (of hair), weakness	職	819 page 178
瞬	SHUN (a short time; to wink, to twinkle, to flicker)	臨	880 page 191
礎	SO; ishizue, foundation, cornerstone	藩	HAN, Japanese feudal clan or domain
穫	KAKU (to reap, to harvest)	覆	FUKU (to upset, to overturn, to cover, to wrap, to hide, to shelter)
簡	KAN, simplicity, brevity, conciseness; (letter, book)	観	367 page 88
糧	RYŌ (food, provisions)	贈	ZŌ; oku(ru), to present as a gift

鎖	SA (hasp; to shut, to close); *kusari*, chain	類	534 page 121
鎮	CHIN (to calm, to quiet, to tranquilize; to suppress)	顕	KEN (bright, clear, distinguished, manifest; to show, to manifest)
離	RI; *hana(reru)* (v.i.), *hana(su)* (v.t.), to separate, to part, to divide, to keep apart	翻	HON; *hirugae(ru)*, to flutter; *hirugae(su)*, to wave (v.t.); to change (one's mind)
難	853 page 185	騎	KI, suffix for counting horsemen; (cavalry, saddle horse; to ride, to mount)
題	464 page 107	騒	SŌ; *sawa(gi)*, noise, disturbance; *sawa(gu)*, to make a noise, to make a disturbance
額	748 page 164	験	600 page 135
顔	179 page 50	闘	TŌ (to fight)

19 STROKES

瀬	*se*, shallows, rapids	簿	BO (notebook)
爆	BAKU (to burst, to explode)	繰	*ku(ru)*, to reel (thread, etc.), to gin (cotton), to turn over (pages, etc.)
璽	JI (Imperial seal)	臓	ZŌ (entrails)

識	627 page 140	願	368 page 88
譜	FU, music, musical score; family record, genealogy	髄	ZUI, marrow, pith
警	KEI (to warn, to caution, to guard against; smart, agile)	鯨	GEI; *kujira*, whale
鏡	378 page 90	鶏	KEI; *niwatori*, chicken
霧	MU; *kiri*, mist, fog, spray	麗	REI; *uruwa(shii)*, fine, lovely, beautiful, elegant, graceful
韻	IN, rhyme, (echo, taste, elegance)		

20 STROKES

懸	KEN, KE (to hang, to suspend; to offer a reward; to be anxious; to depend on)	議	581 page 131
欄	RAN, column (of a newspaper, etc.); railing	護	604 page 135
競	379 page 90	譲	JŌ; *yuzu(ru)*, to hand over, to concede to, to yield to, to reserve
籍	SEKI, census register, membership	醸	JŌ (to brew)

鐘	SHŌ; *kane*, bell	騰	TŌ (to rise, to ascend, to leap)
響	KYŌ; *hibi(ki)*, sound, echo, vibration; *hibi-(ku)*, to echo, to vibrate, to affect		

21 STROKES

艦	KAN (warship)	顧	KO; *kaeri(miru)*, to look back, to reflect upon oneself, to think of, to heed
躍	YAKU (to leap, to jump, to rise, to go up)	魔	MA, devil, demon, evil spirit
露	RO (to expose, to lay bare; to be exposed, to come to light); *tsuyu*, dew		

22 STROKES

驚	KYŌ; *odoro(ki)*, surprise; *odoro(ku)*, to be surprised or frightened, to marvel (at)

23 STROKES

襲	SHŪ; *oso(u)*, to attack; to succeed to; to make a surprise visit	鑑	KAN (model, pattern, example)

PROPOSED CHANGES
in the List of General-Use Characters

Characters to Be Added

厄	YAKU, misfortune, calamity, ill luck 4 strokes	亭	TEI, restaurant, arbor, cottage; suffix used in stage names 9 strokes
汁	JŪ; *shiru*, soup; sap, gravy, juice 5 strokes	挑	CHŌ (to challenge, to make advances to) 9 strokes
朴	BOKU (simple and honest, unsophisticated) 6 strokes	洪	KŌ (flood; great) 9 strokes
戻	*modo(su)*, to return (v.t.), to vomit; *modo(ru)*, to return (v.i.) 7 strokes	俸	HŌ (stipend, salary, rations) 10 strokes
杉	*sugi*, Japanese cedar, cryptomeria 7 strokes	宵	SHŌ; *yoi*, early evening 10 strokes
尚	SHŌ (to respect, to hope, to desire; still, indeed; old) 8 strokes	桟	SAN, frame (of a *shōji*, etc.), crosspiece, cleat, bolt 10 strokes
披	HI (to open) 8 strokes	酌	SHAKU, serving *sake*, helping (a person) to *sake* 10 strokes
泥	DEI; *doro*, mud, mire 8 strokes	竜	RYŪ, dragon 10 strokes
斉	SEI (in good order, equal, the same; to arrange, to manage) 8 strokes	偵	TEI (to inquire secretly into, to spy on) 11 strokes

堀	*hori*, moat 11 strokes	釣	*tsuri*, angling, fishing with a rod and line; change (money) 11 strokes
据	*su(eru)*, to set, to lay, to place 11 strokes	渦	KA; *uzu*, whirlpool, eddy, vortex 12 strokes
殼	KAKU; *kara*, shell, valve, husk, nut-shell, cast-off skin 11 strokes	僕	BOKU (servant), I, me (used by men) 14 strokes
涯	GAI (end, extremity, limits, water's edge) 11 strokes	壤	JŌ (earth, soil) 16 strokes
渓	KEI (ravine, gorge, valley) 11 strokes	矯	KYŌ (to correct, to make straight, to redress) 17 strokes

Additional Readings

and

Simplified Writings

個	10 strokes page 135 (603)	個	KO KA (additional reading)
燈	16 strokes page 112 (485)	灯	TŌ; *hi* (additional reading) 6 strokes simplified writing

Characters to Be Dropped

又	2 strokes page 192	朕	10 strokes page 232
丹	4 strokes page 194	遞	10 strokes page 236
且	5 strokes page 197	堪	12 strokes page 246
奴	5 strokes page 199	脹	12 strokes page 251
迅	6 strokes page 206	煩	13 strokes page 257
但	7 strokes page 206	虞	13 strokes page 258
劾	8 strokes page 214	頒	13 strokes page 260
附	8 strokes page 220	寡	14 strokes page 261
唐	10 strokes page 230	箇	14 strokes page 263
悦	10 strokes page 231	罷	15 strokes page 268

謁	15 strokes page 269	嚇	17 strokes page 273
導	15 strokes page 269	爵	17 strokes page 274
鍊	16 strokes page 273	濫	18 strokes page 275
隸	16 strokes page 273	璽	19 strokes page 276

SYLLABARY

Katakana and Hiragana

ア *a*	⁻ ア	あ *a*	⁻ ㅏ あ
イ *i*	ノ イ	い *i*	し い
ウ *u*	ˋ ㇴ ウ	う *u*	ˋ う
エ *e*	⁻ ㅜ エ	え *e*	ˋ ㇗ え
オ *o*	⁻ ナ オ	お *o*	⁻ ㅏ おお
カ *ka*	フ カ	か *ka*	つ カ か
キ *ki*	⁻ ニ キ	き *ki*	⁻ ニ きき
ク *ku*	ノ ク	く *ku*	く
ケ *ke*	ノ ㇄ ケ	け *ke*	し に け

コ *ko*	フコ	こ *ko*	`こ
サ *sa*	一十サ	さ *sa*	一ささ
シ *shi*	`丶シ	し *shi*	し
ス *su*	フス	す *su*	一すす
セ *se*	フセ	せ *se*	一十せ
ソ *so*	`丶ソ	そ *so*	`ンそ
タ *ta*	ノクタ	た *ta*	一十たた
チ *chi*	ノ二チ	ち *chi*	一ち
ツ *tsu*	`丶ツ	つ *tsu*	つ
テ *te*	一二テ	て *te*	一て
ト *to*	丨ト	と *to*	丶と

ナ na	一 ナ	な na	一 ナ た な
二 ni	一 二	に ni	し に に
ヌ nu	フ ヌ	ぬ nu	し め ぬ
ネ ne	` ラ ネ ネ	ね ne	し れ ね
ノ no	ノ	の no	ノ の
ハ ha	ノ ハ	は ha	し に は
ヒ hi	一 ヒ	ひ hi	て ひ
フ fu	フ	ふ fu	` ら ふ ふ
ヘ he	ヘ	へ he	ヘ
ホ ho	一 ナ オ ホ	ほ ho	し に に ほ
マ ma	フ マ	ま ma	一 二 ま

ミ *mi*	` `` ミ	み *mi*	ス み
ム *mu*	∠ ム	む *mu*	ー む む
メ *me*	ノ メ	め *me*	し め
モ *mo*	ー ニ モ	も *mo*	し も も
ヤ *ya*	フ ヤ	や *ya*	つ つ や
ユ *yu*	フ ユ	ゆ *yu*	い ゆ
ヨ *yo*	フ ヲ ヨ	よ *yo*	` よ
ラ *ra*	ー ラ	ら *ra*	` ら
リ *ri*	｜ リ	り *ri*	い り
ル *ru*	ノ ル	る *ru*	る る
レ *re*	レ	れ *re*	｜ れ れ

ロ	丿 ロ ロ	ろ	ろ ろ
ro		*ro*	
ワ	丿 ワ	わ	し わ
wa		*wa*	
ヲ	一 二 ヲ	を	一 そ を
o		*o*	
ン	丶 ン	ん	丿 ん
n		*n*	

Sound Changes and Kana Combinations

ガ	ga	ギ	gi	グ	gu	ゲ	ge	ゴ	go
ザ	za	ジ	ji	ズ	zu	ゼ	ze	ゾ	zo
ダ	da	ヂ	ji	ヅ	zu	デ	de	ド	do
バ	ba	ビ	bi	ブ	bu	ベ	be	ボ	bo
パ	pa	ピ	pi	プ	pu	ペ	pe	ポ	po
キャ	kya	キュ	kyu	キョ	kyo	シャ	sha	シュ	shu
ショ	sho	チャ	cha	チュ	chu	チョ	cho	ニャ	nya
ニュ	nyu	ニョ	nyo	ヒャ	hya	ヒュ	hyu	ヒョ	hyo
ミャ	mya	ミュ	myu	ミョ	myo	リャ	rya	リュ	ryu
リョ	ryo	ギャ	gya	ギュ	gyu	ギョ	gyo	ジャ	ja
ジュ	ju	ジョ	jo	ビャ	bya	ビュ	byu	ビョ	byo
ピャ	pya	ピュ	pyu	ピョ	pyo				

INDEX OF READINGS

THIS INDEX contains an alphabetical listing of all Japanese readings given in the body of the book. *On* readings are in small capitals and *kun* readings in italics. Main reference numerals indicate pages. Such page references are followed by: (1) an *a* or a *b*, indicating that a given character is to be found in the left- or right-hand column, or (2) a numeral in parentheses, indicating the number of the character as used in the listing of the 881 essential characters. When readings include *okurigana* these are not indicated by parentheses, since they can be found under the individual characters. In most cases where different *okurigana* are added to the same root pronunciation of a character, all readings appear under one entry.

— A —

A 亜 206a
abiru 浴 161(732)
abura 油 119(522)
agaru, ageru 上 19(20)
ageru 揚 248a
AI, *aisuru* 愛 82(339)
AI 哀 222a
ai 相 105(452)
aida 間 26(58)
aji 味 118(516)
aka, akai 赤 22(35)
akarui 明 43(141)
akatsuki 暁 248b
akeru 明 43(141)
aki 秋 32(89)
aki, akiru 飽 260b
akinau 商 101(431)
akiraka 明 43(141)
AKU 悪 45(152)
AKU 握 248a
ama 尼 199a

amai 甘 200a
amari, amaru, amasu 余 160(728)
ame 雨 23(42)
ame 天 38(119)
ami 網 263b
amu 編 157(714)
AN 行 29(73)
AN 安 45(153)
AN 暗 45(154)
AN, *anjiru* 案 83(340)
ana 穴 201a
anadoru 侮 213b
ane 姉 97(413)
ani 兄 54(199)
ao, aoi 青 22(36)
aogu 仰 201a
arai 荒 227a
arasoi, arasou 争 105(451)
aratamaru, aratameru 改 86(359)
aratani 新 66(256)

arau 洗 225a
arawareru, arawasu 現 135(602)
arawasu 表 76(309)
arawasu 著 183(843)
areru 荒 227a
aru 有 119 (523)
aruku 歩 42(136)
asa 朝 38(118)
asa 麻 245b
asai 浅 146(655)
ase 汗 205a
ashi 足 20(29)
asobu 遊 80(326)
ataeru 与 194b
atai 価 127(563)
atai 値 229a
atama 頭 73(294)
atarashii 新 66(256)
ataru, ateru 当 73(290)
atatakai 暖 256b
ateru 充 202a

297

305